4/18

DIABETES
DIAGNOSIS AND MANAGEMENT

By Emily Mahoney

Portions of this book originally appeared in *Diabetes* by Barbara Stahura.

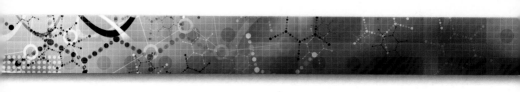

Published in 2018 by
Lucent Press, an Imprint of Greenhaven Publishing, LLC
353 3rd Avenue
Suite 255
New York, NY 10010

Designer: Deanna Paternostro
Editor: Jennifer Lombardo

Library of Congress Cataloging-in-Publication Data

Names: Mahoney, Emily Jankowski, author.
Title: Diabetes : diagnosis and management / Emily Mahoney.
Description: New York : Lucent Press, 2018. | Series: Diseases and disorders | Includes bibliographical references and index.
Identifiers: LCCN 2017033873 | ISBN 9781534562851 (pbk.) | ISBN 9781534562325 (library bound book)
Subjects: LCSH: Diabetes–Treatment. | Diabetes–Diagnosis.
Classification: LCC RC660 .M235 2018 | DDC 616.4/62–dc23
LC record available at https://lccn.loc.gov/2017033873

Printed in the United States of America

CPSIA compliance information: Batch #CW18KL: For further information contact Greenhaven Publishing LLC, New York, New York at 1-844-317-7404.

Please visit our website, www.greenhavenpublishing.com. For a free color catalog of all our high-quality books, call toll free 1-844-317-7404 or fax 1-844-317-7405.

CONTENTS

Illness is an unfortunate part of life, and it is one that is often misunderstood. Thanks to advances in science and technology, people have been aware for many years that diseases such as the flu, pneumonia, and chicken pox are caused by viruses and bacteria. These diseases all cause physical symptoms that people can see and understand, and many people have dealt with these diseases themselves. However, sometimes diseases that were previously unknown in most of the world turn into epidemics and spread across the globe. Without an awareness of the method by which these diseases are spread—through the air, through human waste or fluids, through sexual contact, or by some other method—people cannot take the proper precautions to prevent further contamination. Panic often accompanies epidemics as a result of this lack of knowledge.

Knowledge is power in the case of mental disorders, as well. Mental disorders are just as common as physical disorders, but due to a lack of awareness among the general public, they are often stigmatized. Scientists have studied them for years and have found that they are generally caused by hormonal imbalances in the brain, but they have not yet determined with certainty what causes those imbalances or how to fix them. Because even mild mental illness is stigmatized in Western society, many people prefer not to talk about it.

Chronic pain disorders are also not well understood—even by researchers—and do not yet have foolproof treatments. People who have a mental disorder or a disease or disorder that causes them to feel chronic pain can be the target of uninformed

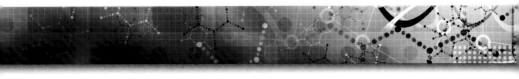

opinions. People who do not have these disorders sometimes struggle to understand how difficult it can be to deal with the symptoms. These disorders are often termed "invisible illnesses" because no one can see the symptoms; this leads many people to doubt that they exist or are serious problems. Additionally, people who have an undiagnosed disorder may understand that they are experiencing the world in a different way than their peers, but they have no one to turn to for answers.

Misinformation about all kinds of ailments is often spread through personal anecdotes, social media, and even news sources. This series aims to present accurate information about both physical and mental conditions so young adults will have a better understanding of them. Each volume discusses the symptoms of a particular disease or disorder, ways it is currently being treated, and the research that is being done to understand it further. Advice for people who may be suffering from a disorder is included, as well as information for their loved ones about how best to support them.

With fully cited quotes, a list of recommended books and websites for further research, and informational charts, this series provides young adults with a factual introduction to common illnesses. By learning more about these ailments, they will be better able to prevent the spread of contagious diseases, show compassion to people who are dealing with invisible illnesses, and take charge of their own health.

INTRODUCTION

A NOT-SO-SWEET DISEASE

Amazing technology allows doctors to treat, manage, and cure more diseases than ever before. From genetic testing to scans such as X-rays, technology allows doctors and technicians to look inside the human body in ways that were not possible even a few years ago. For many centuries, however, doctors had to depend on their knowledge of the human body and limited technology to make diagnoses. This was difficult because doctors did not know nearly as much as they do today, and their diagnoses were frequently inaccurate.

Despite their limited knowledge, even thousands of years ago, doctors noticed that some of their patients were always hungry, and even though they ate large amounts of food, they did not gain any weight. These patients often felt sleepy and weak, and some even fell unconscious. Even stranger, though, was that they suffered from a horrible thirst that no amount of liquid seemed to satisfy, and they had to urinate often, sometimes passing more than 10 quarts (9.6 liters) a day—an amount that would fill nearly five large soda bottles.

Doctors also noticed that these patients' urine smelled extremely sweet. Doctors in ancient India called it "honey urine" and saw "the attraction of flies and ants to the urine of those affected by this ailment."[1] In 17th-century Europe, doctors tasted the urine of these patients and found it to be sugary.

Because of these things, this mystery illness came to be known as sugar disease. Sadly, people who suffered from this disease died quickly because there was no known treatment or cure for their strange and unexplained symptoms.

Today, due to advanced medical knowledge, there is a name for sugar disease: diabetes mellitus, more commonly known as diabetes. Although diabetes is a serious and potentially deadly disease, people who are diabetic can live long, productive lives if they take care of themselves. Thomas Edison, the creator of the light bulb and many other inventions, had diabetes and lived to age 84. Laura Ingalls Wilder, who wrote the Little House on the Prairie books, lived until age 90 despite having diabetes. Many famous people today live well with this disease. Among them are filmmaker George Lucas, actress Halle Berry, and singer Nick Jonas. Even top athletes have

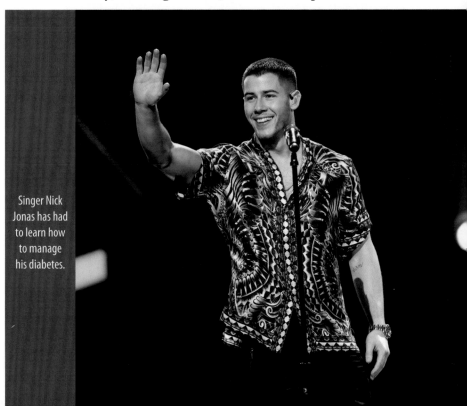

Singer Nick Jonas has had to learn how to manage his diabetes.

diabetes, including NFL quarterback Jay Cutler, baseball player Adam Duvall of the Cincinnati Reds, and Max Domi of the NHL's Arizona Coyotes.

However, even though diabetes can now be managed, having the disease is not so sweet. The Centers for Disease Control and Prevention (CDC) said, "Overall, the risk for death among people with diabetes is about twice that of people without diabetes of similar age."[2] People with diabetes often die from heart disease, and their risk of stroke is two to four times greater than for someone without the disease. Nearly three-fourths of adults with diabetes have high blood pressure or take prescription medications to control high blood pressure. Kidney failure, blindness, and blood circulation problems in the toes, feet, and legs (which can require amputation) are also common complications, particularly in people who are not able to control their diabetes well.

Living with Diabetes

Fortunately, modern medicine has brought hope to many people with diabetes. Unlike in centuries past, the cause of diabetes is now well-known, and many medicines and other treatments can help people with diabetes control their illness. Some of them must take insulin several times a day, but others do not, depending on what type of diabetes they have. They all must be careful with their nutrition and watch their weight, monitor their blood sugar frequently, and stay active, but they can often live energetic, productive lives as well.

Two people who lived a very long time after being diagnosed with diabetes in childhood were Robert and Gerald Cleveland, brothers who lived in Syracuse, New York. They developed diabetes shortly after the discovery of insulin in 1921, and while Gerald passed away in 2009 at the age of 93 and Robert passed away in 2010 at the age of 89, they both lived long, relatively healthy lives.

They said their mother, Henrietta, carefully taught them how to care for themselves so they could stay healthy. "The doctor prescribed the diet I should be on, and my mother was most careful about sticking to it," Robert Cleveland said. "There were very few carbohydrates, a quart and a half of milk every day, and there were lots of vegetables and proteins."[3]

Another remarkable diabetes success story was Gladys Dull, who passed away in 2008 at the age of 91. She had been taking insulin since 1924, just a few months before she turned seven. She calculated that she had more than 60,000 insulin shots since 1924. Furthermore, she said she had survived so well and so long with diabetes because she remained active most of her life and had always eaten a healthy diet. "When I was younger, I did everything—horseback riding, cycling, snowmobiling, motorcycle riding—I always stayed active,"[4] she said. Gladys very carefully determined her portions of food and remained on a similar diet her whole life, which meant her insulin requirements did not change much. "I give my mother credit for that," she said. "She was strict with me, and I thank her for it now."[5]

The Cleveland brothers and Gladys Dull did an excellent job of controlling their diabetes, even though for much of their lives they did not have the gifts of the medical technology and medications that exist today. This shows that with proper care, the battle with diabetes can be won through daily hard work. Today, research into this illness continues, and people who are diagnosed with diabetes have a better chance than ever of surviving, and surviving well, for many years.

CHAPTER ONE

DEFINING DIABETES

Doctors have known about diabetes for thousands of years. In 1552 BC, an Egyptian doctor named Hesy-Ra noted that some of his patients had a disease that caused them to lose weight and urinate often. Over time, doctors began to learn more about how to diagnose and treat the disease, although their limited knowledge meant they sometimes made mistakes. For instance, doctors believed for a long time that horse-back riding decreased people's need to urinate. In the 1800s, some doctors thought eating large amounts of sugar would cure the disease; today, they understand that this makes the problem worse. The development of modern technology and medication, especially insulin, has made it easier than ever for people to control their diabetes, but researchers are still trying to find a way to help people avoid getting it in the first place.

According to the International Diabetes Federation, the number of people with diabetes around the world has risen from 108 million in 1980 to 415 million in 2017, some of whom do not even know they are living with this disease. That number is expected to keep climbing and reach 642 million by 2040. The World Health Organization (WHO) has declared diabetes one of the leading health hazards for the 21st century, and according to a study by the CDC, diabetes mellitus is the seventh leading cause of death in the United States.

In the past, doctors thought horseback riding was a treatment for some of the symptoms of diabetes. Today, doctors know this is untrue.

From 1997 to 2003, the number of Americans diagnosed with diabetes rose by an astounding 41 percent. By 2007, 8 percent of all the people in the United States—24 million—had diabetes, and today, the CDC puts that number at more than 12 percent—about 29.1 million. Furthermore, 25 percent of adults do not yet realize they have this disease, which means they do not know how to properly take care of themselves. Researchers say the diabetes epidemic will continue to grow worse, since more than one-third of Americans over the age of 20 are believed to have a condition called prediabetes, or high blood sugar not yet at diabetic levels. These people have a high likelihood of developing full-blown diabetes.

This epidemic is creating serious problems, especially for children. In the past, diabetes was uncommon in kids. Today, however, about 208,000 young Americans have diabetes.

Epidemic Explanations

One reason so many children and adults now live with diabetes or face its threat in the future is because of another epidemic now underway in the United States: being seriously overweight. More than two out of three Americans are overweight or obese, and about one in three young Americans ages six to nineteen are considered to be overweight or obese. Many of them will develop diabetes, since obesity increases the chances of developing at least one form of diabetes, which is called type 2 diabetes. Too much fat on someone's body, especially around the waist and abdomen, harms the process by which muscles can absorb glucose. Since diabetes occurs when glucose absorption is poor or nonexistent, being overweight can contribute to the development of diabetes.

However, there are other reasons for the diabetes epidemic that researchers have not yet identified. Type 1 diabetes is also on the rise in children, and this type has nothing to do with weight. Experts are unsure why both types of diabetes are on the rise in children, especially since it seems that biological sex—sometimes inaccurately referred to as gender—and race play a role. According to Dr. Barbara Linder, senior advisor for childhood diabetes research at the National Institute of Diabetes and Digestive and Kidney Diseases (NIDDK), "The differences among racial and ethnic groups and between genders raise many questions. We need to understand why the increase in rates of diabetes development varies so greatly and is so concentrated in specific racial and ethnic groups."[6] A study published in 2017 in the *New England Journal of Medicine* found that the rate of type 2 diabetes increased the most for young Asian Americans, while Hispanics were the most affected by an increase in the rate of type 1 diabetes. Type 2 increased more in girls ages 10 to 19, but type 1 increased more in boys of all ages.

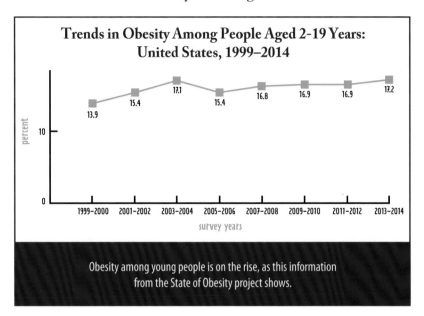

Obesity among young people is on the rise, as this information from the State of Obesity project shows.

Developing Diabetes

Diabetes is a chronic illness, which means it lasts throughout a person's life. It is not contagious. Diabetes occurs because the body cannot properly use the sugar that comes from food. The body gets most of its quick energy from a kind of sugar called glucose, and it pulls glucose out of food during digestion. The process of digestion breaks down food into tiny parts that can be absorbed by the bloodstream. Diabetes results when something happens to disrupt part of this process.

When a person begins eating, digestion also begins. Saliva starts the complex process of breaking down a bite of food even before it leaves the mouth. Swallowing food sends it down the esophagus and delivers it to the stomach, where strong natural acids called gastric juices continue breaking down the food into smaller and smaller pieces.

The intestines are next in line in the digestion process. An average adult human intestine is 27 to 30 feet (8 m to 9 m) long, divided into the small and large intestines. Food traveling all that way has plenty of time to break down into the tiniest, most basic forms a body can use, including molecules of proteins, carbohydrates, fats, and vitamins. One important kind of carbohydrate is the sugar called glucose, which keeps muscles moving and creates important chemical reactions in the body by providing instant energy.

Glucose is also the only energy source for the brain. It is absorbed through the intestinal walls into the bloodstream, and then it travels to every part of the body.

The pancreas is a flat gland located behind the stomach. It is about the size of a hand. Inside the pancreas are thousands of cell clusters called islets, which contain a special kind of cell called beta cells. The beta cells create insulin, which is a hormone that combines with glucose to help glucose move into all the cells in the body and give them energy so they can do their jobs well. A healthy pancreas produces just the right amount of insulin around the clock, based on the amount of glucose circulating in the bloodstream. When glucose is in the bloodstream, it is called blood sugar.

However, if the pancreas cannot make insulin or if the body cannot use the insulin it produces, the glucose cannot get into the cells. It stays in the bloodstream, keeping the blood sugar levels high and causing damage to the organs in the body. For instance, the eyes of a diabetes patient can be damaged by high blood sugar causing blockages in the tiny blood vessels or preventing enough oxygen from reaching the eyes. This can lead to blindness. Diabetes can cause the kidneys to fail so they cannot properly eliminate waste products from the

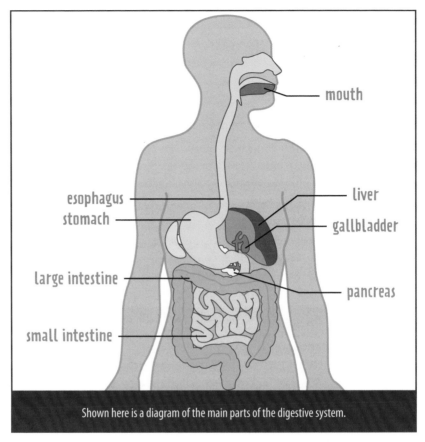

mouth

esophagus

stomach

liver

gallbladder

large intestine

small intestine

pancreas

Shown here is a diagram of the main parts of the digestive system.

body, which eventually leads to death. Diabetes also harms the nervous system by causing a condition called neuropathy. When neuropathy affects the nerves in the feet or legs, they become numb. This can lead to serious foot infections and even amputation of the feet or legs.

Diabetes affects millions of Americans as well as millions of other people around the world. There are several different categories of diabetes, but some are much more common than others.

The Most Common Type

About 95 percent of adults with diabetes have type 2. With this type of diabetes, the pancreas can make insulin, but the body cannot use it properly, so

Is Sugar Really to Blame?

Many people have the mistaken idea that eating too much sugar causes diabetes. Since diabetes used to be called sugar disease and glucose is often called blood sugar, it is easy to see the reason for this mistake. However, evidence shows that simply eating a lot of sugar does not cause diabetes.

According to family practitioner John Messmer, "A much bigger problem is that people are substituting refined sugar for fresh food and consuming sugary foods rather than whole grains, fruits and vegetables. Whole grain bread is better than donuts, whole grain cereal is better than sugary kids' cereals, and fresh fruit is better than syrup laden canned fruit."[1]

In fact, eating too much of anything—carbohydrates, fats, or proteins—can cause people to become overweight, and being overweight can cause diabetes. For overall health, eating a healthy diet with moderate amounts of a wide variety of wholesome foods is best.

1. John Messmer, "The Lowdown on Sugar: Is Sugar as Unhealthy as Everyone Claims?," The Diet Channel, October 25, 2006. www.thedietchannel.com/the-Low-down-on-sugar.htm.

glucose cannot get into the cells. This condition is called insulin resistance. The blood glucose builds up to dangerous levels in the blood and starts to produce symptoms of diabetes.

In the past, most people with type 2 diabetes were adults, so it used to be called adult-onset diabetes. However, as more children began developing this version of diabetes, that term has fallen out of use.

Type 2 diabetes can take many years to develop. People in this developing stage are called prediabetic—their blood glucose levels are higher than normal but not yet in the diabetic range. They are becoming insulin resistant and will develop diabetes unless they take steps to stop the process.

People with type 2 have a strong genetic tendency to develop diabetes. This means they often have one or more relatives who also have type 2. However, other causes also play a big role. Some things people can control, such as being obese and having an inactive lifestyle; others they cannot, such as their race or sex.

The association between type 2 diabetes and being overweight is so strong that people are sometimes surprised to meet a person with type 2 diabetes who is not overweight. Experts believe actress Halle Berry was misdiagnosed in 1989. She was young and in good shape, so after she fell into a diabetic coma, her doctor assumed it was type 1. In 2007, she announced, "I've managed to wean myself off insulin, so now I'd like to put myself in the Type 2 category."[7] Her statement angered many people because it created the idea in some people's minds that people with type 1 diabetes could cure themselves with a certain diet. However, it is impossible for someone with type 1 to stop taking insulin; they will die if they do. Dr. Ronald Kahn, head of the Integrative Physiology and Metabolism section of the Joslin Diabetes Center at Harvard University, said, "She was diagnosed in her early 20s, and at that age it's sometimes difficult to know at the beginning if it's Type 1 or 2 ... Because she is thin and healthy, her physician initially probably thought that she had Type 1, though in African-Americans there is an increased risk for Type 2."[8] Some people believe Berry has a rare type that shares characteristics of both 1 and 2, but doctors have not confirmed this.

Many times, people with type 2 diabetes can bring their illness under control by losing weight and maintaining a healthy diet and getting more exercise. Sometimes they have to take insulin as well, but not always. However, although they can control the effects of the disease, there is currently no cure.

Some people are not able to control their diabetes or do not realize the terrible consequences of not controlling it. A woman named Becky Allen remembered her grandmother and her great aunt, who developed type 2 in middle age and did not eat a healthy diet. In fact, they so loved sugary foods, they would eat too much of them and then manipulate their insulin to make up for the rise in the blood glucose levels. This is a dangerous thing to do. According to Allen,

> As they aged and their bodies manifested the cumulative results of denial—the heart disease, excess weight, progressive loss of vision, the terribly long healing process from any casual injury or broken bone (of which there were many), poor circulation, and the attendant terror of some related amputation—they came too late to any recognition of how the choices they had made impacted their health.[9]

A rise in obesity, sometimes brought on by an inactive lifestyle, has contributed to the rise in diabetes.

The Role of Race

Various ethnic groups in the United States have different rates of diabetes, mainly due to cultural, societal, and environmental reasons. Genetics may play a role, but more research is needed to determine exactly how it affects people's risk of developing diabetes. Many experts believe genes are only part of the issue; the other part is the economic inequality many people of color face. This includes factors such as poor diet, housing segregation, and poverty.

According to the American Diabetes Association (ADA):

• Native Americans have the highest rates of diabetes not only in the United States, but also in the world. This means the disease and its complications are major causes of death and health problems for them. About 16 percent of Native American people have diabetes. Amputations, a complication of diabetes, are three to four times higher in Native Americans than in other ethnic groups.

• African Americans are almost twice as likely to have diabetes than whites. One-third of the 2.3 million African Americans who have diabetes do not know it, which means they are already beginning to suffer from its complications without treatment.

• Latinx people have twice the rate of type 2 diabetes as whites, and about 13 percent of Latinx people have been diagnosed with diabetes. About 14 percent of Mexican Americans in the United States have type 2 diabetes.

A Different Type of Disease

When someone's pancreas cannot make insulin, the person has type 1 diabetes. This type of diabetes occurs mainly in children, so it used to be called juvenile diabetes. However, as more cases have been found in adults, it is more commonly called type 1. About 5 percent of Americans with diabetes have this type. According to the Juvenile Diabetes Research Foundation, that is as many as 3 million people, with about 125,000 of those being age 19 and under.

Type 1 diabetes is an autoimmune disease, which means the immune system makes a mistake and begins attacking healthy body parts. Normally, the immune system produces antibodies that destroy viruses and bacteria that get into the body. For instance, when someone gets a cut on their hand, the immune system immediately starts making antibodies that rush to the cut to prevent infection.

However, with an autoimmune illness, the immune system goes haywire. No one knows why, but it mistakenly sees healthy cells as an enemy and attacks them. When it destroys the beta cells in the pancreas, the body can no longer produce any insulin at all, causing type 1 diabetes.

Alyssa Brandenstein of Evansville, Indiana, was diagnosed with type 1 right around her 13th birthday. She had been an energetic, straight-A student all through school, but then she began to notice strange symptoms. "I was always tired, school was harder to understand, and I just wanted to go to sleep all the time. I didn't feel happy,"[10] she said.

Then, she suddenly lost a lot of weight over a couple of weeks, and "there was a big change in her,"[11] her mother Mindy said. Alyssa's doctor ordered a blood test; the results indicated that she had diabetes, and she developed a condition called diabetic ketoacidosis, which can be life-threatening if not treated. Her family rushed her to the hospital, where she was treated for three days in January 2007. While she was there, she and her family received intense training on how to deal with this new situation.

When Alyssa first got sick, she was scared because she did not know what was wrong with her. However, when she got her diagnosis of type 1 diabetes, she was relieved to have an answer. "I was happy, too, because I knew I would get better," she said. "And I had lots of people to help me."[12] Today, with proper care, Alyssa is leading much the same life she did before her diagnosis.

People with type 1 diabetes must receive insulin from outside sources—generally in the form of insulin shots or through a pump that delivers

People who have Type 1 diabetes often rely on insulin injections to get the insulin their body is not able to make on its own.

insulin to their bodies—several times each day to replace the natural insulin their bodies are no longer making. For that reason, type 1 is sometimes called insulin-dependent diabetes.

Rare Forms of Diabetes

There are two forms of diabetes that are extremely rare. They are called monogenic forms because they are caused by a mutation, or abnormal change, in one gene. Generally, these forms of diabetes are inherited from a parent with the same gene mutation. The other forms of diabetes are polygenic, which means more than one gene as well as a person's environment is responsible for the disease. Monogenic forms of diabetes account for only about 1 to 5 percent of all diabetes cases.

The first monogenic form of diabetes is neonatal diabetes mellitus (NDM), which occurs in babies within the first six months after they are born. In about half the children with NDM, the disease goes away but may return later in life. This group is said to have transient NDM. The other half has permanent NDM, which is with them for the rest of their life.

The second monogenic form is maturity-onset diabetes of the young (MODY). In most people who have it, MODY appears in the teenage or early adult years, although sometimes it is not diagnosed until later. They have the same symptoms as people with the more common types of diabetes, but they are milder; some people do not show symptoms at all. It is often misdiagnosed as either type 1 or type 2 diabetes, so sometimes people refer to MODY as type 1.5, although this term is more commonly used to refer to latent autoimmune diabetes in adults, or LADA. People with MODY are generally not overweight and do not have the other risk factors associated with polygenic forms of diabetes. They can typically treat their disease with special pills instead of insulin, but the treatment depends on which gene mutation has caused the disease.

Type 1.5 and Gestational Diabetes

Two types of diabetes are less well-known: type 1.5 and gestational. Adults who are diagnosed with diabetes but are not overweight, have very little resistance to insulin, and do not immediately need insulin treatment are said to have latent autoimmune diabetes in adults (LADA), or type 1.5 diabetes. Sometimes people who have LADA are misdiagnosed with type 2 diabetes. About 15 percent of people with diabetes have this type, and most people who are diagnosed get it after age 30. According to Dr. M. Regina Castro, "Many researchers believe LADA … is a subtype of type 1 diabetes. Other researchers believe diabetes occurs on a continuum, with LADA falling between type 1 and type 2 diabetes."[13]

Another relatively rare type of diabetes is called gestational diabetes. Gestation or gestational refers to the time of pregnancy. Therefore, gestational diabetes happens when a woman is pregnant, and it can happen even if she did not have diabetes before her pregnancy. If left untreated, this can be harmful to the mother as well as the baby. About 7 percent of pregnant women develop this condition. Gestational diabetes disappears after the baby is born, although more than half of the women who develop this type while they are pregnant will develop type 2 diabetes later in life.

All types of diabetes occur when something goes wrong with the pancreas and its ability to produce insulin or the body's ability to use insulin in the proper way. This serious illness is affecting more and more people in the United States and around the world. Fortunately, modern medicine has developed many new treatments and medications that can help people with diabetes live better and longer lives.

CHAPTER TWO

DIABETES DIAGNOSIS

The symptoms of type 1 diabetes are generally severe, but some people are unaware that diabetes is the reason why they suddenly do not feel well. Twenty-nine-year-old Matt Frith was diagnosed with diabetes in college, a month before his 19th birthday. He knew something was wrong but was not sure what. He lost about 10 pounds (4.5 kg) over the course of a few weeks, was thirsty all the time, and would do nothing but sleep when he was not studying. He said,

> Between the thirst, fatigue, sweet/sugary smelling urine, and other symptoms, your body does an amazing job of trying to tell you what is wrong. I knew uncontrolled type 2 diabetes would cause extreme thirst and would even joke with friends that the reason I was drinking so much water was because I had diabetes, never thinking that at 6'1" and 135 pounds I could possibly have diabetes, despite experiencing all of the symptoms.[14]

Not knowing that type 1 diabetes has the same symptoms as type 2 but has nothing to do with weight, Frith looked for other explanations, such as his diet. He noticed that the more often he ate carbohydrates, the more nauseous he would feel. This was because the body turns carbohydrates into glucose and he was no longer able to process that glucose, but he did not know that at the time. When he visited his doctor's office for a routine checkup, they did a blood test and found that his glucose levels were dangerously high—more than 720 ml/dL (milligrams per deciliter). Knowing what the real problem was allowed him to control his diabetes properly, and today he lives a healthy and active life.

On the other hand, type 2 diabetes creeps up slowly over decades. As someone becomes more overweight and less active, the insulin produced by their pancreas becomes less able to help flush excess glucose out of the body. Often, a person can be prediabetic and have this faulty glucose tolerance for many years with no outward symptoms. However, even though the blood

It is better to be safe than sorry, so anyone who is experiencing the symptoms of diabetes should speak to their doctor as soon as possible. A simple blood test can be done to determine what the problem is.

glucose level is not high enough to be in the diabetic range, it is higher than the healthy range and can begin causing damage to every cell in the body. When diabetes is finally diagnosed, harm may have already been done to the eyes, kidneys, and other organs.

The symptoms of diabetes are now fairly well-known. This is important because the sooner the illness is diagnosed, the sooner treatment can begin.

Type 1 and 2 Clues

When the human body senses something is not working right, it will try to find a way to fix the problem. When the body cannot absorb all the glucose traveling in the bloodstream, it pulls the extra sugar, along with water, out of the blood and puts it in the urine. Then, it gets eliminated in large quantities, many times day and night. This means a person with type 1 diabetes will have to urinate very frequently.

As a person with diabetes continues to urinate too much, the body loses water and begins to dehydrate, just like a sponge drying up. This is a dangerous condition, since water makes up a large percentage of the human body. The brain is 70 percent water, the lungs are 90 percent water, and so is nearly 83 percent of the blood. As too much water leaves the body, the person becomes very thirsty and keeps drinking more liquid to try to quench their thirst.

Since the body is eliminating a lot of glucose in the urine, its usual source of energy from food is very low. This causes it to start breaking down muscles and fat to take the energy stored in them. This can quickly make a person with diabetes dangerously thin and very sick. People with uncontrolled diabetes lose weight very fast without trying. When singer Nick Jonas was diagnosed with diabetes in 2005, he lost 20 pounds (9 kg) in two weeks. However, since the glucose the body takes from its muscles and fat does not have insulin to help it enter the cells, the body's cells will still be starving for energy. This makes a person feel hungry much of the time and continue losing weight, despite frequently eating large amounts of food.

Extreme thirst is one of the major symptoms of diabetes.

Due to all these conditions, a person with undiagnosed or uncontrolled type 1 diabetes will often feel extremely weak. The muscles and the brain cannot get the energy they would normally get from glucose, and as a result, the person feels tired and run-down.

Some people with type 1 diabetes may experience what is called diabetic ketoacidosis (DKA). In this condition, too much of the fat in the body breaks down in order to supply the energy a person would normally get from blood glucose. This forms chemicals called ketone bodies that accumulate in the blood and cause nausea, abdominal pain, and vomiting. Then, as glucose levels rise to very high levels and more water is removed from the blood, the blood becomes very thick and cannot circulate well through the body. The combination of all these things causes extreme drowsiness and loss of consciousness. If this situation is not quickly treated, DKA can become fatal.

In addition, diabetes harms the white blood cells, which help the body heal and prevent infections. Therefore, having diabetes means infections of the skin, gums, and urinary tract heal very slowly. Blurry vision can also occur because as levels of blood sugar rise and fall, the eyes swell and shrink. Since they cannot easily adjust to these changes, the vision blurs as a result.

Diabetes can also harm the nervous system by causing a condition called neuropathy. There are two types: autonomic neuropathy, which mainly affects involuntary body functions such as blood pressure, digestion, and sweat regulation, and small fiber neuropathy, which damages nerves that control feelings of pain and temperature sensitivity. Both types happen when the blood vessels that send blood to the nerves die as a result of not getting enough oxygen and nutrients. When neuropathy damages the nerves in the feet or legs, they can become numb, tingly, or very sensitive to touch. This can lead to serious infections and even amputation of the limbs. Neuropathy takes a long time to develop, often 10 years or more, and symptoms may not appear for a long time, even though damage to the body is already occurring. The symptoms can be treated, and controlling diabetes can keep them from becoming worse, but neuropathy does not have a cure.

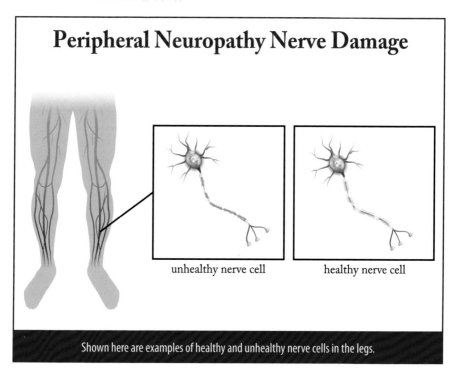

Peripheral Neuropathy Nerve Damage

unhealthy nerve cell   healthy nerve cell

Shown here are examples of healthy and unhealthy nerve cells in the legs.

A serious complication of diabetes is cardiovascular disease, which can cause heart attacks and strokes. Cardiovascular conditions affect people with diabetes nearly twice as much as people without it. Diabetes can alter some of the substances in the blood, which can cause the blood vessels to narrow or clog up in a process known as atherosclerosis, or hardening of the arteries.

Many people with type 2 diabetes do not experience symptoms for a long time, but when symptoms are present, they are the same as type 1. If someone with type 2 diabetes ignores the symptoms for too long, they can suffer complications and eventually die.

Increased Risk

About 23 percent of adults in the United States have a group of risk factors, called metabolic syndrome, that can increase the chances of developing diabetes as well as heart disease and stroke. According to the American Heart Association, someone must have three of the following five symptoms to be diagnosed with the syndrome:

- obesity in the abdomen (the waist measures more than 40 inches for men and more than 35 inches for women)
- a higher than normal level of the fat in the blood called triglycerides
- a lower than normal level of "good" cholesterol, called HDL (high density lipoprotein)
- higher than normal blood pressure
- higher than normal fasting blood glucose (the level of glucose present in the blood when a person has not eaten for several hours)

Type 1.5 and Gestational Diabetes Clues

People with type 1.5 diabetes are generally adults whose diabetes develops slowly over time. For this reason, it is often mistaken for type 2 diabetes, but it is an autoimmune disease like type 1; it is not influenced by a person's weight. These people may be thin and active, yet it is difficult for their bodies to control glucose levels. In its early stages, type 1.5 does not require insulin, but this often changes after at least six months.

Gestational diabetes often either has no symptoms, or the symptoms are mild and not threatening. It may be difficult for a pregnant woman to identify whether she has it without talking to a doctor. Actress Salma Hayek said that when she had gestational diabetes, she felt nauseous throughout her pregnancy, but since nausea is a normal pregnancy symptom, she was unsure at first whether something was wrong. If a pregnant woman does have symptoms, they may include blurry vision, increased thirst and urination, fatigue, nausea and vomiting, and weight loss even

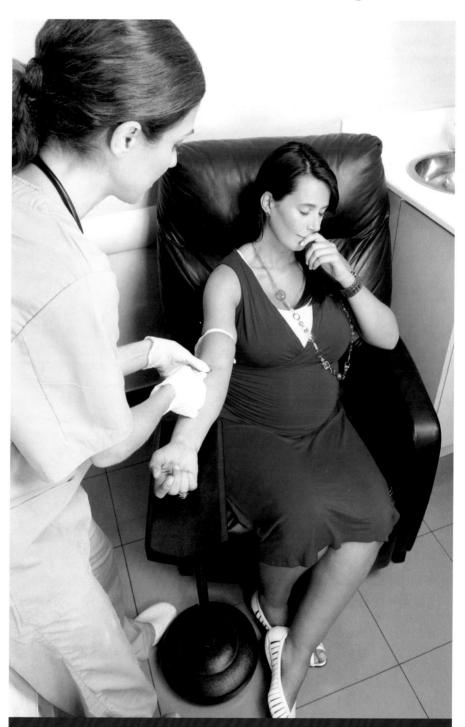

Gestational diabetes generally goes away once the baby is born, but it can be a serious pregnancy complication if it is not managed correctly. Diagnosis through a blood test is the first step toward proper management.

with increased appetite. Typically, blood glucose levels return to normal after the baby is born, although developing gestational diabetes is a hint that a woman may develop type 2 diabetes later in life. Although the symptoms are mild, gestational diabetes must be treated not only for the mother's sake, but also to protect the baby from developing harmful conditions. If left untreated, the baby may be born with a high birth weight, which makes delivery more dangerous for both the baby and the mother. Additionally, right after birth, the baby may have extremely low blood sugar and temporary breathing problems.

Diabetes Diagnosis

Doctors use several tests to check for diabetes and prediabetes in their patients. All of them require that blood be drawn and tested in a medical lab. The first one is called the fasting plasma glucose (FPG) test; it is the method doctors prefer because it is easy, convenient, and less expensive than other tests. The FPG measures a person's blood glucose after fasting (eight hours of not eating or drinking anything except water); generally, the person does not eat anything after 10:00 p.m. and gets the test done before breakfast the following morning. If the fasting glucose level is 99 mg/dL or below, the person does not have diabetes. If the level is 100 to 125 mg/dL, the person has prediabetes, and if it is 126 mg/dL or higher, the doctor will perform the test again to confirm the results. If the same results appear in the second test, the person has diabetes.

The oral glucose tolerance test (OGTT) is another measure of blood glucose. After eight hours of fasting, blood is drawn and its glucose level is measured to provide a baseline number. Then, the person drinks a special beverage of glucose dissolved in water. Over the following two hours, blood is periodically drawn again to check the glucose level. As with the FPG, depending on the glucose level, doctors can tell whether a person has prediabetes, diabetes, or neither. The OGTT can be used to diagnose gestational diabetes as well.

A third test is the random plasma glucose test. The blood glucose level is checked regardless of when the person last ate. This test is useful for diagnosing diabetes in people whose blood sugar levels are dangerously high and who need treatment immediately, but it will not give a good reading for someone whose situation is less urgent. If the person tests negative for diabetes but has all the symptoms, the doctor will likely have the patient undergo either the FPG or the OGTT to verify the diagnosis.

Treating Diabetes

Successfully treating diabetes requires different strategies for the various types, and people with the illness must do what is best for them within those strategies. No one except the patient and their doctor can decide what the best course of action is. However, two things are crucial: monitoring blood glucose levels and, in many cases, using insulin and perhaps other medications to manage symptoms.

Even people who are able to carefully control their glucose can experience a wide range in levels, depending on many variables such as what they have eaten, their activity and stress levels, illness, and the amount of sleep they get. Therefore, most people with diabetes check their blood sugar several times a day and monitor the levels closely. People who can keep their blood glucose at ideal levels will feel better and have more energy, and they can also prevent or hold off diabetic complications longer. According to the National Institutes of Health (NIH), ideal blood glucose levels for someone without diabetes are 70 to 130 mg/dL before meals and less than 180 mg/dL two hours after the start of a meal. People with diabetes try to keep their blood sugar levels within these ranges.

The number of times blood glucose levels are tested is determined by the type of diabetes, the kind of treatment used, and how stable the person's glucose levels typically are. People who are taking insulin generally test before each meal and at bedtime to see if they need to adjust their insulin dose. People with diabetes cannot know how well they are controlling their blood glucose, no matter how well they feel, unless they do these frequent checks. For most people with type 2 diabetes, testing just twice daily—before breakfast and dinner—gives enough information if blood glucose levels are fairly stable.

Checking blood glucose can also be helpful at other times—for instance, after trying a food the person does not normally eat—to see how it affects glucose levels. Before exercise is another good time. The test will reveal whether eating before exercising is a good idea or if exercise can be used to bring down the blood sugar level. Finally, if a diabetic person has been experiencing unstable glucose levels and is about to drive, a test beforehand will reveal if hypoglycemia, or low blood glucose, might be a problem. Hypoglycemia can cause the brain to not function as well as it normally does, which can be dangerous while driving.

Checking blood sugar levels requires a tiny sample of blood, generally from a fingertip. It is taken with a lancet, which is a tiny needle that is often built into blood glucose meters. The lancet penetrates the skin just enough to get a drop of blood. Using the side of a finger is recommended, since the sides are less sensitive than the tips. Using a different finger each time is also advised to avoid soreness or sensitivity in one finger.

The blood sample is placed on a test strip in the

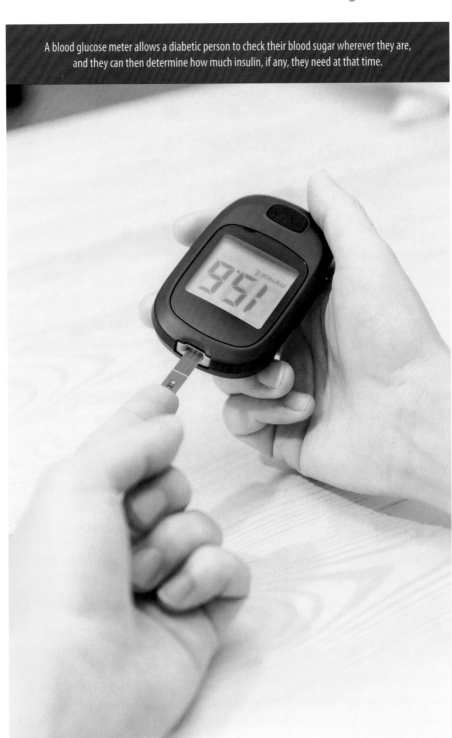

A blood glucose meter allows a diabetic person to check their blood sugar wherever they are, and they can then determine how much insulin, if any, they need at that time.

meter. The strip is coated with special chemicals that react with the glucose. After a moment, the glucose meter displays the blood sugar level as a number. Knowing their blood sugar level allows the person to decide whether they need to take further action.

Blood Sugar Levels

Another important test for blood glucose is performed by a doctor to show a person's blood sugar levels over the past two or three months. It is called the hemoglobin A1c (HbA1c) test.

Hemoglobin, a protein that carries oxygen in the bloodstream, attaches to glucose to form hemoglobin A1c. By testing for this, a diabetic person and the physician can look back in time and see if blood glucose levels were well controlled, which is important for helping people avoid complications such as blindness or neuropathy. Also, the results will let the doctor and patient know whether treatment is working by showing improvement in glucose levels. If the treatment is not working, they can adjust it as needed.

Replacing Insulin

The major treatment for type 1 diabetes is replacing the insulin the person's body can no longer make. Some people with type 2 take insulin, too, but often they can regulate their blood sugar just by eating healthy foods, exercising, losing weight, and not smoking. Several times daily, the patient receives insulin through injections they give themselves or through a small computerized pump that automatically injects insulin under the skin at the right times. These insulin pumps are becoming increasingly common. Most models are worn outside the body on a belt or waistband. One version that can be implanted

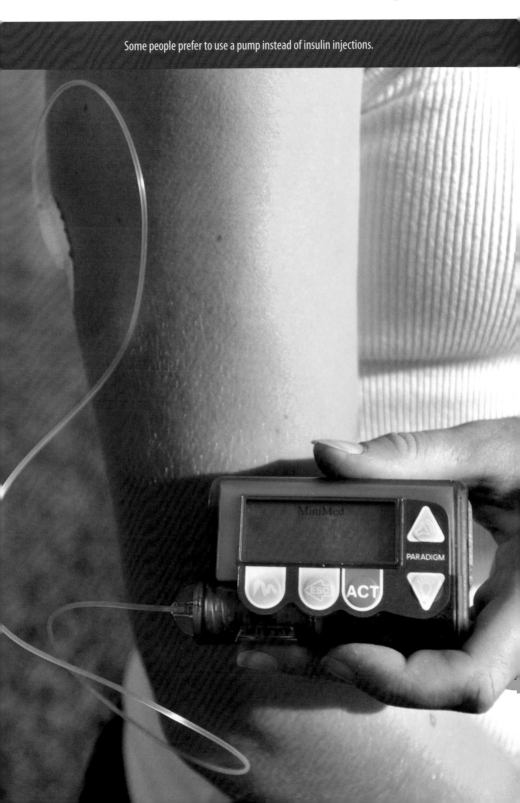

Some people prefer to use a pump instead of insulin injections.

How Do Insulin Pumps Work?

Some people choose to wear an insulin pump instead of injecting insulin because they feel it helps them better manage their symptoms. Insulin pumps have also been proven to deliver insulin more effectively than injections, and they can help stabilize blood sugar levels as well. After using an injection pen for almost 10 years, Matt Frith switched to a pump for exactly those reasons. He found the pump gave him more flexibility and control over his blood sugar by letting him change the settings whenever he needed to, such as when he was exercising, eating high-fat foods such as pizza and ice cream, or had a cold—all of which can affect the body's ability to absorb glucose. In contrast, an injection gives a set amount of insulin every time. Additionally, Frith said, "Being a technically driven person, I also like being able to see a graph of the sensor glucose reading whenever I want, which provides me with insight into trends and how my body reacts to different foods and at different times of the day."[1]

Insulin pumps are worn outside the body, but they are connected to thin tubing called a catheter. This catheter runs from the pump under a person's skin, and the insulin runs from a reservoir inside the pump into a person's body. The reservoir needs to be monitored to ensure that there is enough insulin in it, but generally, the pump will alert its wearer with a beeping noise if the insulin level is low. Typically, people disconnect the pump when they are showering or swimming, because while pumps are water resistant, they are not fully waterproof. Some people also buy cases to protect the pump, similar to buying a case for a cell phone.

Frith described the effect switching to a pump had on his life:

> My diabetes management is now less distracting; instead of giving myself an injection at every meal, I measure my blood sugar and then press a few buttons on the pump and that is it—no untucking my shirt or rolling up my sleeve to give myself an injection, making it more discreet. The big concern I had before I got the pump was having something always attached to me, but that took less than three days to get accustomed to.[2]

Some people may find pumps helpful, while others may have trouble with them. A person with diabetes who is considering getting a pump should discuss the options with their doctor.

1. Matt Frith, e-mail interview by author, July 17, 2017.

2. Matt Frith, e-mail interview.

inside the body was approved for use, but the company that made it stopped production in 2007. In the waistband model, insulin is delivered inside the body through a small tube called a catheter. The implanted version goes under the skin and is refilled with insulin every few months. Some people are trying to convince medical product companies to make the implanted version again.

When insulin as a treatment for diabetes was first created, it was made from pig and cow pancreases, so it was impure and low quality. Fortunately, modern medicine can now produce synthetic, or man-made, insulin of the highest quality and purity from genetically engineered bacteria. It is identical to the insulin created by the human pancreas.

This manufactured insulin is also made in four types that act differently in the body in three ways. First is onset, or how long the insulin begins to work after it is injected. Second is peak, or how long it takes for the insulin to reach maximum effectiveness after it is injected. Third is duration, or how long the insulin remains effective.

The four basic types of insulin each have their own onset, peak, and duration. It is common for people with diabetes to use these four types of insulin in various combinations to better manage their illness. The rapid-acting type begins working in 10 to 30 minutes, peaks in 30 to 120 minutes, and has a duration of 3 to 5 hours. The short-acting type begins working in 30 to 60 minutes, peaks in 2 to 5 hours, and has a duration of up to 12 hours. The intermediate-acting type begins working in 90 minutes to 4 hours, peaks in 4 to 12 hours, and has a duration of up to 24 hours. Last, the long-acting type begins to work in about 1 to 4 hours, has a minimal peak, and has a duration of 24 hours.

Other Treatment Options

Many people with diabetes take oral medications, either alone or along with insulin, to better manage their condition. These medications come in various categories, and each works differently. They can have side effects, including upset stomach, low blood glucose, weight gain, liver failure, headache, and fluid retention. They must be taken as prescribed and under a doctor's care. Studies have shown that diabetes complications might be prevented by these oral medications. This is especially true when the person taking them also eats a healthy diet and gets adequate regular exercise.

Complications

Thinking about the possible complications of diabetes can be frightening. No one wants to believe they could go blind, have a foot or leg amputated, or suffer from kidney failure. However, understanding the complications of diabetes soon after diagnosis is the best way to begin preventing them. Maintaining a healthy diet, exercising regularly, and monitoring blood glucose as often as needed are the best first steps.

Additional steps must be taken to delay or prevent the onset of diabetic complications. No one should smoke, but smoking can have additional negative effects on people with diabetes. Smoking damages the heart and narrows the blood vessels, which are already under stress from diabetes. Blood pressure must be kept low. Hypertension, or high blood pressure, puts a strain on the body and can cause eye disease to progress faster. Losing weight and exercising, limiting salt for some people, and medications can all lower blood pressure.

People with diabetes should have annual physicals and regular eye exams to spot early signs of

Smoking can increase the chances that a person
with diabetes will experience complications.

complications. They should also get good dental care. Gum infections are common in people with diabetes. Flossing, brushing, and regular dental exams can prevent them. Feet can be a victim of diabetes because cuts and blisters can easily become infected and be slow to heal. Feet should be washed daily in warm water, dried gently, and moistened with lotion everywhere except between the toes, which are areas that are more prone to infection caused by moistness. Feet should be checked daily for blisters, cuts, swelling, and redness.

For people with diabetes, the first step in taking care of themselves is receiving a diagnosis with one of the reliable tests available today. Once the diagnosis has been confirmed, they can work with a doctor to determine the best method of keeping their illness under control.

CHAPTER THREE

DIABETES TREATMENT AND MANAGEMENT

Diabetes can be a difficult disease to live with, and managing it requires consistent, responsible self-care. Many people with diabetes have lived long, productive lives because they take proper care of themselves. This means they eat healthy food, exercise consistently, and monitor their blood sugar to ensure that it is within an appropriate range. Diabetes expert Sheri Colberg interviewed many people with the disease when she was writing her book, *50 Secrets of the Longest Living People with Diabetes.* They showed her that "attention to health and lifestyle has a positive effect."[15] In other words, living well with diabetes is all about self-management.

Colberg herself has had type 1 diabetes since she was four. While diabetes has complicated her life, it has not stopped her from living it to the fullest. She is an author, lecturer, professor, exercise physiologist, and expert on exercise and diabetes. She is also a mother, wife, and enthusiastic exerciser. Even with diabetes, "the world is still open to you," she said. "But it is work, and you have to be aware and plan ahead, like taking your blood glucose meter and medications along wherever you go."[16]

Diabetes management has several key components: weight, nutrition, exercise, and adequate sleep. Programs are available in many places to help people learn how to manage their diabetes properly.

Learning About Diabetes

Once Colberg was old enough to understand her diabetes, she was afraid she would die at a young age from its complications. In the 1970s and 1980s, when she was growing up, that is what the medical literature told her. Today, those fears are gone. New research has brightened the picture and vastly improved the lives of people with diabetes, yet this diagnosis may still be frightening and confusing at first. Diabetes is a serious, chronic disease that can lead to terrible complications. Therefore, it is important that newly diagnosed people are educated about diabetes self-management. Ideally, this program is presented by their health care teams, and many resources are also available elsewhere from books, the Internet, and support groups.

The main focus of diabetes self-management education and support (DSME/S) is giving people the facts and training needed to maintain physical health. The educational part of the program teaches patients how to check their blood sugar, what and when to eat, how to inject themselves with insulin, how to recognize and treat low and high blood sugar, where to buy diabetes medications and supplies, and how to store them. Often, the family is involved so they can support their loved one in the important task of managing diabetes.

However, once the initial education is done, people with diabetes may find it difficult to continue doing what must be done for their whole lifetime. They may get discouraged or tired of having to check their blood sugar or watch what they eat. As Colberg found out in her own life, often "the problem is not so much the physical issues as the emotional ones. Diabetes crosses the physical body, the psyche [mind], everything."[17]

This is where the "support" part of the program comes in. In this approach, people with diabetes work with their health care team and often with a support group of other people with diabetes to become more self-reliant in managing their illness. Rather than feeling overwhelmed by their disease, DSME/S can help them feel more empowered to handle it safely and well. They learn together how to solve problems they face with their illness and receive support from others who understand what it is like to live with diabetes. In addition, they are more likely to eat right more often, create better exercise habits, and set goals for themselves, such as exercising and eating correctly, that keep them feeling better physically and emotionally. Family workshops or camps for kids with diabetes are also helpful for this kind of support. According to the American Diabetes Association (ADA),

> *DSME/S is reported to reduce the onset and/or advancement of diabetes complications, to improve quality of life and lifestyle behaviors such as having a more healthful eating pattern and engaging in regular physical activity, to enhance self-efficacy and empowerment, to increase healthy coping, and to decrease the presence of diabetes-related distress and depression.*[18]

Weighing In on Nutrition

Fat inside someone's body contributes to diabetes because too much of it interferes with the way insulin operates. However, once diabetes develops, even a small amount of weight loss can help control it.

People with diabetes need a plan that lets them safely choose the right amounts and kinds of food to eat. By using sound guidelines to plan meals and snacks that fit their unique lifestyles, they will be able to better control their blood glucose. In addition to helping them lose pounds or maintain a healthy weight, an eating plan keeps their food balanced with insulin and other medications.

Healthy eating is vital to diabetes management
and is important for overall health as well.

A Deadly Consequence

A deadly trend has developed among some people with type 1 diabetes, particularly young women: They skip insulin to lose weight. However, the results of this foolish practice can be life-threatening.

The first effects of insulin skipping can be nausea, depression, and exhaustion that become worse over time. Eventually, it can have life-threatening consequences. This type of eating disorder is sometimes called diabulimia, and it generally occurs along with one of the more common eating disorders, such as bulimia or anorexia. Eating disorders generally have to do with a person's need to feel control over their body; they do this by controlling what they eat, which leads to an obsession with weight.

In 2016, *Broadly* reported on Rebecca Ryan, a young woman who was hospitalized after skipping her insulin shots:

Rebecca was 19 when she began deliberately withholding insulin to lose weight. Over the next five years, the [weight] dropped off. Eventually, so did her hair. By the time she was 24, she had descended into a spiral of guilt, shame, and unhappiness that only ended when she accepted she wasn't just bad at managing her diabetes—she was suffering from an eating disorder ...

At the beginning [after being diagnosed with diabetes], keeping record of what she ate was kind of fun. She lived with two trainee doctors, and they made a game of it. But soon, Rebecca got sick of her life being measured. "I wanted everything to be perfect, every time I tested I wanted my numbers to be perfect and if they weren't I felt like a failure ... I went to a really weird and dark place. I would avoid doctors' appointments, because I didn't want them to see I wasn't in control. It's awful because you know the consequences of your actions could be [blindness], limb amputations, but none of that stuff seems to matter. I was just at my most vulnerable then, I was so self-conscious. But everyone was telling me I looked great, and that's kind of what gets you."[1]

1. Michelle Duff, "The Diabetic Women Who Skip Insulin to Lose Weight," *Broadly*, December 12, 2016. broadly.vice.com/en_us/article/vb4ezm/it-was-a-weird-and-dark-place-how-women-with-diabulimia-dice-with-death.

A healthy meal plan takes into account the person's likes, dislikes, and food allergies. Creating a meal plan is best done with a dietitian's help. Dietitians are experts in nutrition and healthy eating. They define a healthy diet as one that includes a variety of foods from all the food groups, is high in vitamins and minerals, is high in fiber, and is low in processed foods. A healthy diet also reduces the risk of other health problems, such as heart attack, cancer, and stroke. Generally, a diet that is healthy for people with diabetes is healthy for anyone. With proper planning and attention to portion size, people with diabetes can eat the same healthy and delicious foods their families and friends do.

A Healthy Plate

In 2011, the U.S. Department of Agriculture (USDA) released new dietary guidelines for Americans to follow to make sure they are eating the correct amount of different food groups. Called MyPlate, the guidelines can be used to help everyone—not only people with diabetes—follow a well-balanced and nutritious eating plan.

These guidelines are based on science, and they recognize that all people have their own food needs according to their age and level of activity. For instance, a grown man who works in an office and does not exercise needs less food than another man who is a marathon runner. A teenage girl needs a different amount of food and nutrients than her younger brother. Women in their 30s have different nutritional needs than women in their 70s. All these things are true whether or not someone is diabetic, but diabetes requires more attention to the details of eating.

MyPlate

The new guidelines illustrate the five food groups that are the building blocks for a healthy diet by using an easy-to-follow picture of a place setting for a meal. Food is broken down into five categories: fruits, vegetables, grains, protein, and dairy. The guidelines give suggestions about the best foods to eat in each category. For instance, whole grain bread is better than highly processed white bread, and oatmeal is better than sugary cereals. The amount of each food a person should eat depends on their age, sex, and level of activity.

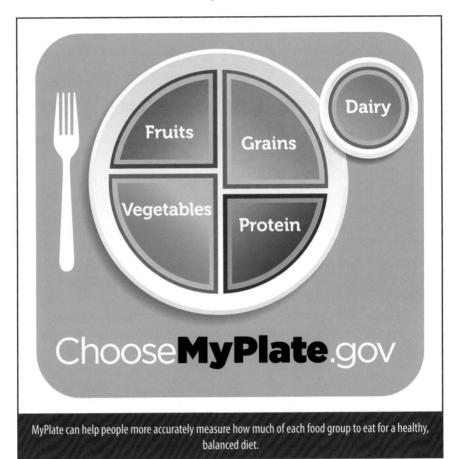

MyPlate can help people more accurately measure how much of each food group to eat for a healthy, balanced diet.

Eating the right amount of food is also important. Too many calories mean weight gain. Underestimating the number of calories in food is easy to do, particularly when portion sizes are large. Learning to closely estimate the correct portion size can be a great help in losing or maintaining weight as well as controlling blood sugar. For instance, the healthy adult portion for a steak is 3 ounces (85 g), or about the size of a deck of cards. One cup of salad greens is similar in size to a baseball. A half-cup serving of ice cream is the size of half a baseball.

Learning the correct portion sizes of foods is a skill that can be mastered and one that is tremendously helpful for anyone wanting to maintain a healthy weight for their lifetime. When Matt Frith was first diagnosed, he used measuring cups at every meal, even those he ate in his college dining hall. Over time, this

Fighting Diabetes and Obesity

Native Americans have some of the highest rates of diabetes in the United States, partially because many of them live in poverty and have less access to healthy foods. To help reduce these rates, many American Indian and Alaska Native communities participated in the CDC's Traditional Foods Project from 2008 to 2014. The project promoted 17 tribal programs that "worked to restore access to local, traditional foods and physical activity to promote health."[1] According to the CDC, the project had several goals:

- *Support traditional, sustainable, evaluable ecological approaches to type 2 diabetes prevention, focusing on local efforts to reclaim traditional foods and physical activity.*

- *Encourage local health practices and policies to increase availability of and access to local, traditional foods and physical activity.*

- *Revive, create, and preserve stories of healthy traditional ways shared in homes, schools, and communities.*

- *Engage community members to improve and sustain activities in health promotion, sharing stories of hope for preventing diabetes and its complications.*[2]

Although the program ended in 2014, the results are archived on the CDC's website, and many Native communities have continued to use what they learned from the project to improve their health.

1. "Traditional Foods Project, 2008–2014," Centers for Disease Control and Prevention, January 26, 2016. www.cdc.gov/diabetes/ndwp/traditional-foods/index.html.

2. "Traditional Foods Project, 2008–2014," Centers for Disease Control and Prevention.

habit helped him learn how to tell by sight what the correct portion sizes were. For people with diabetes, eating at the right times and coordinating medications with food is also necessary. In general, they should eat the same amounts of food at the same times every day whenever possible.

People with type 1 diabetes should not skip meals because they always have insulin in their bloodstream from their injections. Along with meals at regular times, a snack in the midmorning and midafternoon is a good idea. A bedtime snack may also help regulate glucose levels through the night. Weight control might be more of an issue for people with type 2 diabetes, since most of them are overweight. Even a weight loss of 10 percent of body weight can play a large role in reducing the symptoms of diabetes.

Staying Active

Exercise is important for everyone, and for people with diabetes, it is one of the best ways to manage their illness. Regular exercise improves glucose tolerance (so blood sugar can be controlled better with less medication) and lowers cholesterol and blood pressure. It reduces the risk of life-threatening complications of diabetes; strengthens muscles, bones, and the heart; and keeps joints flexible. It can also help people feel happier and more energetic because it reduces stress and causes the brain to produce natural "feel good" chemicals called endorphins.

People do not have to run marathons or ride a bike for hours to get enough exercise. Many little activities, such as taking the stairs or choosing a parking space farther from the door to the mall or school, can add up to big benefits. Vacuuming the house, gardening, mowing the lawn, washing the car, and walking the dog all count as physical activity, especially if done energetically. The Department of Health and Human

Exercise is important for everyone, but it is especially useful for helping people with diabetes regulate their blood sugar levels.

Services recommends a minimum of one hour of physical activity per day.

People who have been inactive for a long time should see a doctor first to see if they are healthy enough to exercise. They should explain what kinds of exercise or activities they want to try. Some might be off-limits because of diabetes. For instance, for people with diabetes who have less sensation in their feet, swimming or biking might be better than walking or running.

Both aerobic exercise and strength training are beneficial to people with diabetes (and to everyone else). Aerobic means "with oxygen;" aerobic exercises such as walking, swimming, or biking at a faster than normal pace get the heart pumping and oxygen flowing through the body to burn calories. Strength training with weights—even small ones—builds muscles, and bigger muscles burn more fat faster.

People should choose an activity they like because they are more likely to continue exercising if they enjoy it. They can also seek out a qualified exercise specialist or personal trainer to learn how to lift weights, use exercise equipment, or do other unfamiliar activities.

It is also important to check with a doctor about the best times to exercise. People who take insulin might need to adjust their doses or wait a while after injecting their insulin before exercising.

Exercise Tips

Few studies have been done about the best time for people with diabetes to exercise. In 2015, the *Journal of Diabetes Science and Technology* published a study that found people with diabetes were more likely to develop hypoglycemia if they exercised after 4 p.m. rather than before 7 a.m. Other studies have found that exercising after meals is better than exercising before them. Everyone's body is

different, so people with diabetes may have to exper-
iment to find out when they feel best after exercising.

Researchers also recommend that people with diabetes learn how to determine the right insulin dosages
before, during, and after exercise. Too much insulin
before a workout can lead to hypoglycemia, while
not enough insulin can cause too-high blood sugar,
or hyperglycemia. Stress and heat can affect the blood
glucose and insulin balance, so these factors must also
be taken into account.

A good idea is to have some carbohydrates available
during exercise in case blood sugar needs to be raised
quickly. Eating carbohydrates helps to prevent hypoglycemia. Exercising with a partner who knows what
to do in case of a diabetic emergency can add a safety
factor as well as make exercise more fun.

Medical Emergencies

Emergencies related to diabetes will eventually happen to everyone who has the illness. People who have
a hard time controlling their diabetes will have them
more frequently than those whose diabetes is more
well-controlled, but even those people can have diabetic emergencies from time to time. These medical emergencies are impossible to predict, and they
can be deadly if the person does not seek immedi-
ate help. A diabetic emergency occurs when glucose
levels are either too low (hypoglycemia) or too high
(hyperglycemia). The best way to prevent or minimize
these situations is to know what a diabetic emergency
is, know how to handle it, and do everything possible
to avoid it.

One common reason for diabetic emergencies is
that even with the best glucose monitoring, the same
dose of insulin can have varying effects at different
times. The effect depends on the kinds and amounts
of food eaten, the amount of exercise and stress, and

Sometimes drinking sugary juice or eating a snack with sugar is needed during a hypoglycemic episode. People who are diabetic often keep these things on hand.

how healthy the person is.

People with type 1 have more frequent swings in blood glucose than people with type 2, so they may experience more emergency situations. Hypoglycemia is the most common emergency condition for people with type 1 because they take insulin or medications that lower blood glucose. In people who do not have diabetes, the body naturally stops releasing insulin before blood glucose falls too low. However, once insulin is injected, its action cannot be stopped. If hypoglycemia continues for too long, the person could have seizures, lose consciousness, or die. Fortunately, once someone learns to recognize the signs, they are able to treat their condition before it becomes too dangerous.

Hypoglycemia Treatments

Having help available when needed is important.

Family members, coworkers, or other trusted people should learn to recognize the symptoms of hypoglycemia and know how to treat it if necessary. Some symptoms of hypoglycemia include dizziness, sweating, feeling shaky or faint, sweating, rapid heartbeat, clumsiness, moodiness, and extreme hunger. However, each person should know their own particular symptoms since everyone reacts differently.

Some people eventually lose their ability to realize they are hypoglycemic. If they miss the early signs, fuzzy thinking may be the first symptom, which means they will not know how to help themselves. It is recommended that these people test blood glucose more frequently, wear a diabetes ID bracelet, and keep a prescription for glucagon nearby. Glucagon is a hormone that, when injected, causes the liver to release glucose, and it also slows insulin release. People with type 1 must know how to inject it and also should train someone, such as a family member or roommate, to inject it in case they are unable to do so.

In a case of severe hypoglycemia, the person must immediately eat or drink a small amount of a carbohydrate that the digestive system can quickly pick up from the bloodstream. Glucose tablets or gel from the pharmacy work well, as do hard candy, raisins, regular soda, 100 percent juice, or candy that does not contain chocolate. These sugars should be kept easily available at all times. About 15 minutes after taking one, blood sugar should be checked. If it is still too low, the person can eat another sugar source or a meal if possible.

Hyperglycemia Treatments

The other diabetic emergency is hyperglycemia, or when blood sugar becomes too high. It is unpredictable, possibly deadly, and happens to all people with diabetes. This is less common than hypoglycemia but still very dangerous. People with types 1 and 2 can

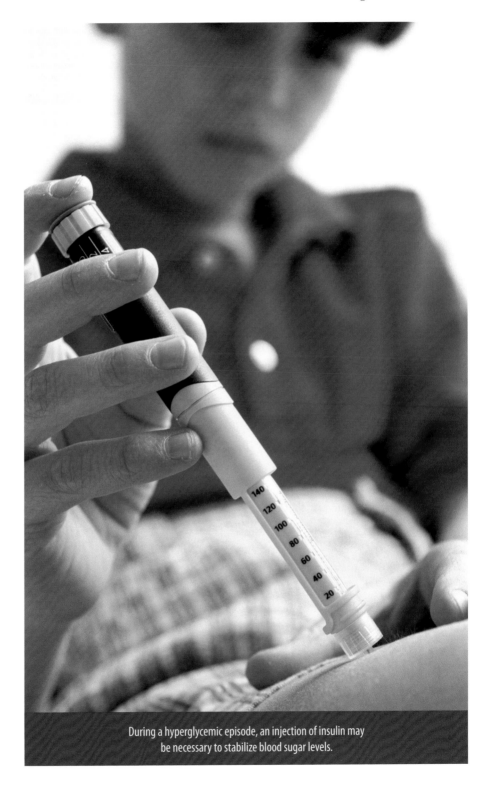

During a hyperglycemic episode, an injection of insulin may be necessary to stabilize blood sugar levels.

suffer from it but react differently.

In type 1, DKA occurs when people do not get enough insulin. The body believes it is starving and breaks down fat to get energy. This causes ketones to form in the blood, and if the body cannot release them through urine, they build up and poison the body. The body also becomes dehydrated because of frequent urination, which only increases the concentration of ketones. As ketones build up to dangerous levels, coma, shock, difficulty breathing, and death can result.

Symptoms generally come on slowly. Early DKA symptoms include increased thirst, frequent urination, and blurry vision. If left untreated, other symptoms can develop, such as nausea and vomiting, weakness, fruity odor on the breath, confusion, and stomach pain.

Someone who is hyperglycemic must have an injection of quick-acting insulin and drink a lot of water or another sugar-free liquid. If the condition does not improve rapidly, the person must seek emergency medical help. People with type 2 diabetes can have hyperglycemia for a long time without realizing it, especially if they have not yet been diagnosed with diabetes. Their glucose level can zoom to extremely high levels, which can lead to coma and death.

Hyperglycemia leads to a condition called Hyperglycemic Hyperosmolar Syndrome, or HHS. It can happen to people who do not use insulin but take oral medicines. HHS symptoms include sleepiness or mental confusion, extreme thirst, hallucinations, dry mouth, loss of vision, and unusually warm skin. Also, the person will have high blood glucose levels. Seeking medical help is important when blood sugar levels are extremely high. The best way to avoid HHS is to check glucose levels at least once a day.

Managing diabetes can be complicated and time-consuming, but it is necessary in order to avoid the terrible complications that can happen as a result of having this illness. Careful management includes blood glucose monitoring, medications such as insulin, regular exercise, and a healthy diet. In addition, studies have shown that laughter and a positive attitude have a good effect on people, including those with diabetes. Laughter produces chemicals in the body that make people feel better in general, which helps make daily life easier and more pleasant. Although laughter is not treatment for diabetic emergencies, it can help keep stress levels low, which is a good way to keep blood sugar at a normal level. Reading a funny book, watching a comedy, or sharing amusing stories with friends are all good ways for people to bring laughter into their lives.

CHAPTER FOUR

COMING TO TERMS WITH DIABETES

While diabetes can produce serious complications, millions of people live with it, and they are still able to have fulfilling, productive lives. They learn how to manage their condition to minimize the possibility of diabetic emergencies, and many of them eventually become so comfortable with having diabetes that they are able to joke about it with others.

"Diabetes doesn't have to hold you back from much of anything," Colberg said, knowing this from her own life as well as from others' experience. "Diabetes can even make you stronger, because you have to take responsibility for yourself."[19]

When people are diagnosed with diabetes, they can feel overwhelmed and frightened. This is why support from friends and family is important. Having someone they can count on generally makes learning about diabetes control easier and less stressful.

What Not to Say

People who do not know much about diabetes may think it is funny to joke about a person's dependence on insulin or make fun of a newly diagnosed person for measuring their food precisely, but these kinds of comments can make a difficult time even harder. Additionally, hearing the same comments repeatedly can be very frustrating, even for people who have had their diabetes under control for a long time.

People who have just been diagnosed with diabetes and are still learning how to control it are likely very aware of all the complications their disease could cause. Friends and family should avoid reminding them of these so the person with diabetes does not feel extra stress. They should also avoid making the person feel bad for the things they have to do to control their diabetes, such as giving themselves injections or measuring their food precisely. Many people without diabetes are scared of getting shots, so they react with horror when they find out some people with diabetes have to do it several times a day. This can make the person with diabetes feel upset, especially since it is something they cannot help; they must do it to stay alive.

People who have had diabetes for a long time and are skilled at managing it may get frustrated when other people try to help them manage it. Generally, advice about diet and exercise is not welcome to people with diabetes unless it comes from their doctor. This means people should avoid asking whether a person with diabetes is allowed to eat something they have on their plate. Even worse is asking whether someone will die if they eat something; although certain foods may contribute to either hyperglycemia or hypoglycemia, someone with diabetes will not instantly die if they eat the wrong thing. People with diabetes also do not enjoy when people who have no medical training try to tell them to eat a specific food or exercise more in order to treat or "cure" their diabetes. They have worked with a doctor to find the combination of diet, exercise, and medicine that works best for them. Additionally, diabetes can never be cured, only controlled.

When people do something enough times, it looks effortless to people who do not do it at all, and this applies to managing diabetes. It may look easy, but

People with diabetes know how to manage their own disease. They do not need or want advice if they have not specifically asked for it.

that management takes lifelong time and effort. For this reason, people should not act like diabetes management is not a big deal, when in fact it is something many people with diabetes have to think about constantly. They may learn how to do it effectively, but it will never be something they can entirely ignore. Additionally, many people without diabetes encourage people with diabetes to get a pump instead of taking insulin injections, in the mistaken belief that a pump manages diabetes without requiring any work from the person it is attached to. In reality, the person with diabetes still needs to tell the pump how much insulin to inject, and pumps require more training than injections. "Many people don't realize the amount of work involved with pumps," said Dr. Andrea Penney of the Joslin Diabetes Center. "Using a pump requires professional training and close diabetes management."[20]

Diabetes Daily gave a list of several comments people with diabetes find particularly annoying:

- *You have diabetes? You don't look that fat …*

- *You take insulin? Oh, you must have the bad kind of diabetes …*

- *Well, that sounds better than something like leukemia …*

- *That's the disease that causes you to lose your legs, right?*

- *I heard you can cure that with diet and exercise …*

- *I eat so much sugar, I'm probably gonna give myself diabetes, too! …*

- *Why don't you get a pump that just manages it for you? …*

- *Are you allowed to eat that? …*

Diabetes During Puberty

Diabetes often gets harder to control during adolescence and puberty. All the hormonal changes underway can make blood glucose and insulin levels swing wildly, no matter how carefully the adolescent with diabetes works to stay within normal levels.

During puberty, growth hormone stimulates bone and muscle mass to grow, and it also works to block insulin. At the same time, as blood sugar falls, another hormone called adrenaline is released into the bloodstream, which triggers the release of stored glucose. The result is that blood glucose can fluctuate up and down very quickly. Adolescents who are diabetic must work extra hard to manage their diabetes, but eating healthy, getting plenty of sleep, and exercising can all help blood sugar levels stay more regulated.

Due to their changing bodies, teenagers must work harder to control their diabetes than either children or adults. It is a good idea for them to check their blood sugar more often.

- *They say _(any random food)_ can level your blood sugars …*

- *You have diabetes? But you look normal …*

- *Well, it's your fault, right, for eating too much and not exercising?*[21]

Some of these comments are well meant, but they are all inappropriate. Instead of shaming or scaring someone with diabetes or offering unwelcome advice, friends and family should support their loved one. One way they can do this is by offering to join them in their diet or exercise changes. This can make the person with diabetes feel like they are not alone, and a healthy diet and regular exercise benefits people without diabetes as well. Another way is by being sympathetic to the fact that managing diabetes is a full-time, never ending job that can sometimes be stressful. Being a good listener and asking if there is anything they can do to help shows love and support and can make things easier for the person with diabetes.

Getting Support

Although caring friends and family do their best to support their loved one with diabetes, it can be difficult sometimes for people without diabetes to understand exactly what their loved one is going through. This is why many organizations offer support groups for people with diabetes. These groups allow people with the disease to meet and exchange stories, tips, and jokes with each other. Having the support of people who are in the situation can make managing the disease seem like a much easier task.

Some diabetes support groups meet in person at places such as a church or community center. There are different kinds of groups for different sets of people; for instance, there may be one group specifically

Assistance Dogs

Assistance dogs for people who are blind, deaf, or have other physical challenges have become a familiar addition to the range of tools that help them live safely. Now, some dogs are being trained to help people with diabetes avoid the danger of low blood sugar. Especially for very young children or people afraid of becoming hypo-glycemic without realizing it, these dogs are proving their worth.

Trainers of these dogs say they are right 90 percent of the time in sensing a dangerous fall in blood glucose even before the person with diabetes is aware of it. When they sense this, they "alert"—jump, run around, pace, or put their head in their owner's lap—to remind their owner to eat some appropriate food to bring glucose levels up to normal. The dog then gets a treat.

While no one yet knows how dogs do this, it is believed they are able to pick up scents created by the chemical change in their owners' bodies.

These hypoglycemic-alert dogs cost around $20,000, and the training of the dog takes about two years, but they can be amazing tools in helping people with diabetes manage emergency situations.

Service dogs can be trained to recognize hypoglycemia and warn their owners of an upcoming issue.

for teens, another specifically for women, a third specifically for Latinx, and so on. The Joslin Diabetes Center offers this advice on finding the group that best fits a person's needs:

> *In order to decide which diabetes support group is best for you, speak with the person running the group.*
>
> • *Inquire about the person's credentials, how he or she sees the purpose of the group, and how it will be run.*
>
> • *Make a list of what you want to get from the group.*
>
> • *Ask specific questions with regard to your goals and purposes.*[22]

Some people may not have in-person diabetes support groups close to them. In this case, they can either start their own group or join one online. In a blog post on the website Diabetes Hands Foundation, Ginger Vieira said,

> *Before you've found the DOC (Diabetes Online Community), living with diabetes can feel very lonely simply because the chances of being able to easily communicate with people who know [what it is] like to live with diabetes are hard to find. In my own life, the people I know locally with diabetes I actually know thanks to the DOC! ... Whether you're a parent of a child with diabetes, the spouse of a loved one with diabetes, or living with any type of diabetes yourself, you can find support in this community.*[23]

A Diabetes Advocate

Today, diabetes does not have to stop people from doing much of anything. With proper planning and

Nicole Johnson (shown here) never let diabetes control her life.

care, combined with the exciting new medical technology available, a person with diabetes can follow their dreams. Diabetes advocates such as Nicole Johnson help people understand diabetes and encourage researchers to learn more about how they can help those who have it.

When Johnson was diagnosed with type 1 diabetes at age 19 in 1993, she had no idea she would later be crowned Miss America in 1999. In fact, her doctors warned her against competing in the pageant because they said the stress would be harmful.

She entered anyway. During the entire pageant, she wore her insulin pump, as she always does, and talked with many people about the illness. Now in her mid-40s, Johnson is a national diabetes consultant for the company that makes her insulin pump. She was a cohost of *dLife*, a weekly television program on CNBC aimed at helping people with diabetes. She has written many articles about living with diabetes, her autobiography, and several cookbooks. She is also a familiar face in Washington, D.C., where she promotes legislation regarding diabetes.

Johnson earned her doctorate in public health in 2013 and was appointed chair of the board of the Diabetes Empowerment Foundation in 2016. When she was diagnosed with diabetes, her doctors told her she should never have children because of the danger diabetes would pose to her and to the baby. Today, however, her daughter Ava is a healthy teenager.

Diabetes has certainly affected Johnson's life, but it has also given her the opportunity to be a role model for empowering people with diabetes. She said, "One's greatest challenge can be one's greatest blessing, physically and psychologically."[24] In that light, she has always not only accepted her diabetes but also found it to be a blessing. By dealing with it honestly and openly, she has created a good career that revolves around it. She has also used the strength and wisdom it has brought her in her family and professional life.

Playing Sports with Diabetes

In the past, people with serious, chronic illnesses were expected—even ordered—to remain inactive out of fear that too much activity would be harmful. They would often also hide their disease as if it were something shameful or hide themselves from the public eye because they believed acknowledging their illness would damage their reputation. Fortunately, as Jay Cutler and other athletes are demonstrating, such beliefs are outdated.

To watch Cutler on the football field, it is impossible to know that the athletic NFL quarterback has type 1 diabetes. His throwing arm is strong; he is energetic and powerful. He is still fast on his feet, and he is working hard to remain that way. Cutler was diagnosed in April 2008 after mysteriously losing 33 pounds (15 kg) the previous fall, along with having severe thirst, fatigue, frequent urination, and unstoppable hunger.

"I was just crushing food," he recalled. "I was eating six meals a day—I'd eat a meal and like 30 minutes later I'd be ready to eat again. Yet I kept losing weight, and they were telling me it was the stress. I was like, 'I'm not that stressed.' I mean, my jeans were falling off my body and I was all pale."[25]

Former Denver Broncos coach Mike Shanahan praised Jay for taking control of his illness. "Jay has met this thing head on," Shanahan said. "I'm really not surprised. I mean, he was diagnosed with a very serious disease, and he has just gone after it and is treating it. He's done a great job of dealing with it. Jay has great discipline."[26]

Now Cutler, who comes from Santa Claus, Indiana, faithfully checks his blood glucose levels and injects

NFL quarterback Jay Cutler was diagnosed
with type 1 diabetes when he was 24 years old.

himself with insulin several times daily. His weight is back up to a healthy level. He says he feels fine and does not experience many highs or lows in his blood sugar.

Today, millions of people have diabetes. They come from all ethnic and social groups. They can be rich or poor, college graduates or uneducated, old or young. However, they all have one thing in common: They can still have good, productive lives. That does not mean it will be easy, because managing and coping with diabetes is hard work. It requires patience and determination. However, oftentimes, coping with a serious illness can make people stronger and more willing to face other challenges.

CHAPTER FIVE

DIABETES IN THE FUTURE

Unfortunately, more people than ever are developing diabetes, so the drive to find better ways to manage and even cure this disease is stronger than ever before. In recent years, diabetes care has improved tremendously because of ongoing research, new medicines, and increased knowledge about how to manage the disease. People who have diabetes also receive better medical care, counseling, and emotional support than in years past.

Many people who are diabetic wish for a future where they do not have to inject themselves with insulin, use a pump, or take insulin through a daily pill. They hope they will no longer need to prick their fingers to get a blood sample to test their glucose levels as well. New devices and advances are making these dreams closer and closer to reality. Many researchers are investigating several new possible treatments for diabetes, including stem cell research, tissue engineering, gene research, and developing an artificial pancreas. The hope is that someday, diabetes will not only be easier to manage, but will also be fully cured.

Using Technology

Improvements in technology have led to improvements in diabetes management. One of these technologically advanced systems is a mobile app called Dexcom G5 CGM (Continuous Glucose Monitoring). To use the app, a small sensor is implanted just below the skin and a transmitter sends data wirelessly from the sensor to the app. The app can then track a person's glucose levels all the time, which eliminates the need for blood testing and lets someone know immediately whether they need to take insulin or eat a snack.

Another new type of technology is the Omnipod System, which is a small, lightweight pump that is designed differently than traditional pumps. Rather than being worn on a belt and delivering insulin through tubes, the Omnipod can be worn right on the skin. A wireless device called a Personal Diabetes Manager (PDM) controls the insulin delivery; it works as long as the person is within five feet of the PDM. Some people prefer the Omnipod because it is waterproof, they do not have to wear the PDM all the time, and the PDM has extra features such as a list of foods and their carbohydrate counts.

Researching Stem Cells

Embryonic stem cells are immature cells in animal embryos that later develop into other cells that make up all the various organs and tissues of the body, such as the heart, eyes, lungs, bones, and pancreas. Early in their development, they are like blank slates, but then a complex process happens in the embryo to make them begin changing into those different kinds of cells. Adults also have stem cells, but they work differently from embryonic stem cells, and they are not used for the same kind of research.

An enormous amount of research has already been done with the pancreas. Scientists have identified the "master" genes in this organ, and some of these master genes tell embryonic stem cells to become beta cells, which create insulin. Some researchers have also been able to grow cells called induced pluripotent stem (iPS) cells, which have the ability to become any kind of cell, just like embryonic stem cells. Researchers at the Mayo Clinic "have successfully generated patient-specific iPS cells and subsequently converted them into glucose-responsive, insulin-producing cells in the laboratory."[27]

In this photo, a scientist examines stem cells under a microscope. Stem cell treatments look promising for people with diabetes.

Growing New Tissue

Tissue engineering is an amazing process that scientists recently developed to help replace damaged parts of the body. Someday they hope to be able to grow various organs, even hearts and lungs, in the lab for people who need transplants. Tissue engineering is still very new, but researchers are making advancements all the time.

Engineered skin is made by taking skin cells from a person who, for instance, has suffered severe burns and cannot regrow enough of their own skin naturally to cover the burned portions. Those skin cells are used to grow pieces of new skin in a lab. The new skin can then be grafted over the burned areas to help them heal.

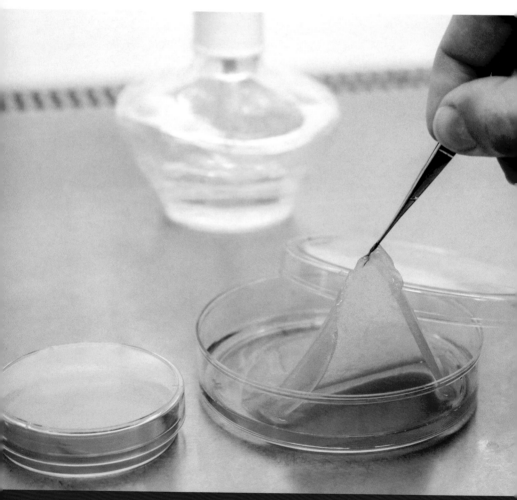

Scientists are now able to grow human skin that can be used to treat various conditions.

It is common for people with diabetes to have cuts or wounds on their feet that do not heal, even after many months of treatment, because their illness damages the skin of the feet and legs. These wounds can become seriously infected, which can lead to amputation. It has been found that tissue-engineered skin can be used to help these wounds heal. Unlike the skin used for some burn victims, this new skin is made from tissues other than the patient's, but it works very well. The doctor carefully cleans the wound and then places the tissue-engineered skin over it. It grafts with the person's skin, and the body restores the injured area. Treating these wounds with tissue-engineered grafts promotes faster healing than other treatments. It is also less risky and less expensive than taking live skin from a donor.

Tissue engineering also presents many opportunities for researchers looking for improved diabetes treatments or a cure. They believe beta cells can eventually be tissue-engineered to replace the damaged or missing ones in the pancreas of a person with type 1 diabetes. These cells would be placed into the person's pancreas, where they could grow and reproduce to make adequate amounts of insulin once again.

Some scientists have already had success creating functional pancreases in mice and rats and hope they will soon be able to do the same for humans. According to *Asian Scientist,*

> *Mouse pancreases grown in rats generate functional, insulin-producing cells that can reverse diabetes when transplanted into mice with the disease, according to researchers at the Stanford University School of Medicine and the Institute of Medical Science at the University of Tokyo.*

> *These findings, published in* Nature, *suggest that a similar technique could one day be used to generate*

matched, transplantable human organs in large animals like pigs or sheep.[28]

Transplanting Islets

The islets of Langerhans are clusters of cells in the pancreas that contain beta cells, which make insulin. There are two types of islet transplant surgeries. In the first, allo-transplantation, islets are carefully removed from a deceased person's pancreas, purified, and transplanted into the pancreas of a person with severe type 1 diabetes. The results are promising but by no means perfect; most people need more than one transplant to feel the positive effects, and only a few hospitals in the United States are allowed to perform them. According to the NIDDK,

> *The goals of the transplant are to help these patients achieve normal blood glucose levels with or without daily injections of insulin and to reduce or eliminate hypoglycemia unawareness—a dangerous condition in which a person with diabetes cannot feel the symptoms of hypoglycemia, or low blood glucose. When a person feels the symptoms of hypoglycemia, steps can be taken to bring blood glucose levels back to normal.*[29]

The other kind of surgery is called auto-transplantation, which can only be performed on type 2 diabetics. In this procedure, the patient's pancreas is removed, then the islets in it are purified and transplanted back into the patient's liver.

As with any transplant, rejection is the greatest risk and problem. When the body senses something inside it that it believes does not belong there, the immune system will attack it in an effort to get rid of it. With type 1 diabetes, the immune system often mistakenly destroys the person's own beta cells, and this can happen again with new islets from someone else.

That is why people who receive any kind of transplant, including islets, must take special drugs, called immunosuppressive drugs, to prevent the body from attacking and destroying the transplanted islets. These drugs must be taken for life. Unfortunately, these drugs can have terrible side effects, including mouth sores, digestive problems, anemia, and high blood pressure and cholesterol levels. Because they suppress the immune system, they make the person more likely to have infections, and they also increase

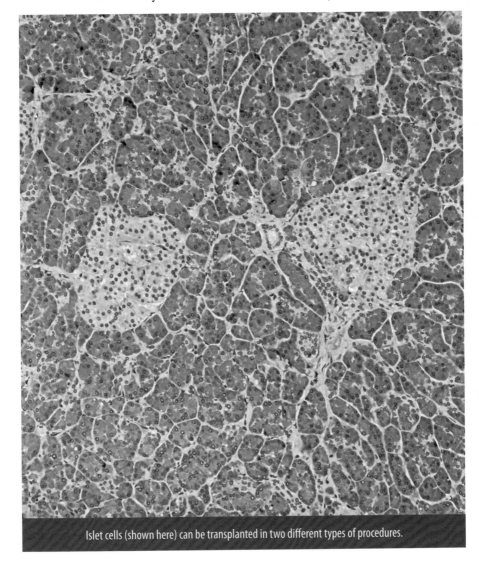

Islet cells (shown here) can be transplanted in two different types of procedures.

An Unusual Remedy

Researcher Annika Axelsson and her team have discovered a surprising treatment for type 2 diabetes: concentrated broccoli sprout extract. The researchers found that sulforaphane, which is a compound that occurs naturally in vegetables such as broccoli, reduced the amount of glucose produced by lab-grown liver cells and appeared to reverse diabetes in rats. To get enough sulforaphane to make a difference, someone would have to eat a very large amount of broccoli sprouts, so the researchers concentrated it—they put a lot of the chemical into a pill or injection form. This way, people could get the chemical without having to eat more broccoli sprouts than they could manage.

When 97 trial volunteers took concentrated broccoli sprout extract for 12 weeks, participants who were obese and having trouble controlling their diabetes showed "significantly decreased fasting blood glucose levels"[1] compared to people who did not take the extract. More research is needed before this treatment can be provided to the general public, but it is a promising start.

Concentrated broccoli sprout extract is being investigated as a possible treatment for diabetes.

1. American Association for the Advancement of Science, "Could Broccoli Be a Secret Weapon Against Diabetes?," *Science Daily,* June 14, 2017. www.sciencedaily.com/releases/2017/06/170614141526.htm.

the risk of cancer. Therefore, people who undergo islet transplantation must first understand the possible severe side effects. Researchers are continuing to look for new and better immunosuppressive drugs with fewer side effects. Their main goal is to help people who receive islet transplants achieve immune tolerance, which would enable them to keep the new islets functioning normally without all the drugs.

Genes and DNA

Both types 1 and 2 diabetes have their roots in a person's genes, which carry deoxyribonucleic acid (DNA), or the basic building blocks of an organism, from one generation to the next. Half of a person's genes come from their mother and half from their father, and human beings have tens of thousands of them. Genes determine whether people have blue, brown, or green eyes; how tall they are; if they go bald; if they have the potential to develop various illnesses; and so on.

To complicate matters, just because a person has a gene linked to a certain disease, that does not mean the person will eventually develop the disease. For instance, if someone has the genes related to type 2 diabetes but maintains a healthy weight and gets enough exercise throughout their life, the disease may never appear.

The study of genes is still very young, so scientists have much to learn about the human genome, or the full collection of human genes. However, one thing they do know is that diseases, including diabetes, are generally caused by multiple genes. Perhaps diseases would be easier to cure if only one gene were responsible.

Janelle Noble is a researcher at Children's Hospital Oakland Research Institute who is building a genetic database of children and families with diabetes. At a meeting of diabetes experts, she said, "If we're going to prevent diabetes we have to know who's likely to get it in the first place. But looking for variants of genes that cause complex diseases is like looking for a needle in a haystack."[30]

Research also suggests that many more varieties of diabetes than types 1, 2, 1.5, and gestational may exist. If this is the case, then the genetic basis for diabetes will be even more complicated than previously believed, and treatment could be much more personalized than it is today. Many researchers studying this are investigating questions such as, of two equally overweight people, why does only one have diabetes?

Understanding genes and DNA through research on mice and rats may one day help scientists find a cure for diabetes.

Or, why do some diabetics still have healthy kidneys even after decades of poor blood sugar levels, while others' kidneys are terribly damaged early on?

A gene therapy developed at Baylor College of Medicine seems to have cured diabetes in mice by turning their liver cells into beta cells that produce insulin. The mice were completely cured of diabetes for at least four months. Since the liver cells came from the mice themselves, antirejection drugs were not needed. While it will be many years before this procedure can safely be used in humans, it is a very promising development.

Could Implantable Pumps Make a Comeback?

In the 1980s, implantable insulin pumps were considered a futuristic piece of technology. Many people wanted them because they hold more insulin than the pumps people currently wear on their belts. They also administer insulin in a faster and more effective way than other pumps or injections. However, the company that made this device stopped making it in 2007, preferring to put its money into researching other kinds of diabetes technology, such as an artificial pancreas. As of 2017, only four people in the United States still use an implantable pump.

An organization called the Implantable Insulin Pump Foundation was launched in November 2016 to raise awareness about how much better they feel implantable pumps are and try to convince companies to start making them again. Although Medtronic, the original company that made them, says it does not have plans to start production again, a San Diego company called PhysioLogic Devices is in the early stages of developing an improved implantable insulin pump. If it passes all the tests that are required before it can be sold, it could be available to people with diabetes within the next few years.

A New Pancreas

An artificial pancreas would revolutionize diabetes treatment. By automatically regulating a person's blood glucose, such a device implanted under the skin would allow people with type 1 diabetes to keep their levels within a normal range.

Scientists are already developing an artificial pancreas and are having some success, although it is not yet ready for widespread use. This human-made pancreas has three parts: a sensor to continually monitor blood glucose, an insulin pump, and a small computer that controls insulin delivery.

Artificial pancreases are just starting to become available for human use. In 2016, the Food and Drug Administration (FDA) approved the first artificial pancreas for people with type 1 diabetes who are 14

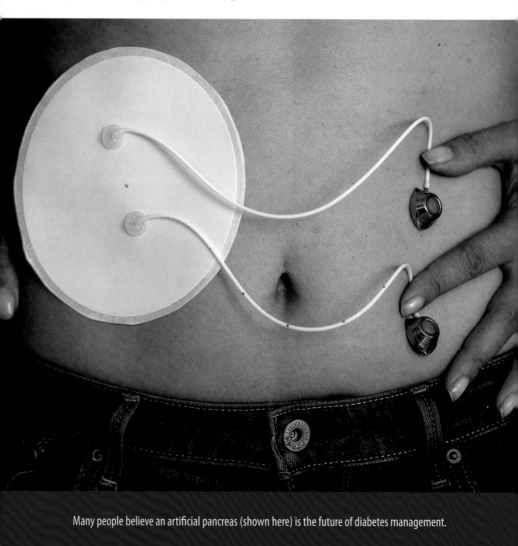

Many people believe an artificial pancreas (shown here) is the future of diabetes management.

or older. According to Diabetes in Control, the device, which is called the MiniMed 670G,

automatically administers or withholds insulin in response to blood glucose measurements, which it takes every five minutes ... The system is made up of a sensor that measures blood glucose under the skin; an insulin pump; an infusion patch that delivers insulin from the pump via a catheter inserted into the skin and a computer chip that uses data to optimize insulin delivery by the minute.[31]

In April 2017, soon after the MiniMed 670G went on the market, a teenager named Claire Bickel became the youngest person to receive one. She will still need to test her blood sugar, but the device will help keep it more stable.

These technological advancements will make controlling diabetes far easier in the future, and eventually, a cure may even be found. However, it will take many more years of research before that dream becomes a reality. Until then, people with all types of diabetes must continue taking care of themselves by watching what and when they eat, taking any required medications, and getting plenty of exercise.

Introduction:
A Not-So-Sweet Disease

1. Lee J. Sanders, "From Thebes to Toronto and the 21st Century: An Incredible Journey," *Diabetes Spectrum*, vol. 15, no. 1, 2002, p. 57.

2. Quoted in Miranda Hitti, "No End in Sight to Rapid Rise in Diabetes," WebMD Medical News, October 26, 2005. diabetes.webmd.com/news/20051026/no-end-in-sight-to-rapid-rise-in-diabetes.

3. Quoted in Richard Perez-Pena, "Diabetic Brothers Beat Odds with Grit and Luck," *New York Times*, February 5, 2006. www.nytimes.com/2006/02/05/nyregion/05diabetes.html.

4. Quoted in Diabetes Health Staff, "After All These Years: 83 Years of Living Well with Diabetes," Diabetes Health, May 29, 2007. www.diabeteshealth.com/after-all-these-years-83-years-of-living-well-with-diabetes-gladys-c-lester-dull/.

5. Quoted in Diabetes Health Staff, "After All These Years: 83 Years of Living Well with Diabetes."

Chapter One:
Defining Diabetes

6. Sean Rossman, "Diabetes Is on the Rise in America's Kids and Experts Don't Know Why," *USA Today*, April 14, 2017. www.usatoday.com/story/news/

nation-now/2017/04/14/diabetes-rise-americas-kids-and-experts-dont-know-why/100469336/.

7. Quoted in Russell Goldman, "Berry's Miracle Cure Probably Misdiagnosis, Say Docs," ABC News, November 6, 2007. abcnews.go.com/Health/DiabetesResource/story?id=3822870.

8. Quoted in Goldman, "Berry's Miracle Cure Probably Misdiagnosis, Say Docs."

9. Becky Allen, "The Banana Pudding Incident," unpublished.

10. Mindy Brandenstein, telephone interview with Barbara Stahura, May 5, 2008.

11. Mindy Brandenstein, telephone interview.

12. Alyssa Brandenstein, telephone interview with Barbara Stahura, May 5, 2008.

13. M. Regina Castro, "Expert Answers: LADA," Mayo Clinic, October 19, 2016. www.mayoclinic.org/diseases-conditions/type-1-diabetes/expert-answers/lada-diabetes/faq-20057880.

Chapter Two:
Diabetes Diagnosis

14. Matt Frith, e-mail interview by author, July 10, 2017.

Chapter Three:
Diabetes Treatment and Management

15. Sheri Colberg, telephone interview with Barbara Stahura, May 29, 2008.

16. Sheri Colberg, telephone interview.

17. Sheri Colberg, telephone interview.

18. "Diabetes Self-Management Education," American Diabetes Association, accessed July 17, 2017. www.professional.diabetes.org/ diabetes-self-management-education.

Chapter Four:
Coming to Terms with Diabetes

19. Sheri Colberg, telephone interview.

20. Quoted in "Insulin Injections vs. Insulin Pump," Joslin Diabetes Center, 2017. www.joslin.org/ info/insulin_injections_vs_insulin_pump.html.

21. Ginger Vieria, "Top 29 Most Annoying Things to Say to People with Diabetes," *Diabetes Daily*, May 2, 2017. www.diabetesdaily.com/ blog/2013/03/top-29-most-annoying-things-to-say-to-people-with-diabetes/.

22. "Finding the Right Diabetes Support Groups," Joslin Diabetes Center, 2017. www.joslin.org/ info/finding_the_right_diabetes_support_ groups.html.

23. Ginger Vieira, "Getting to Know the Diabetes Online Community (DOC)," Diabetes Advocates, September 14, 2013. diabetesadvocates.org/getting-to-know-the-diabetes-online-community-doc-2/.

24. Quoted in David Templeton, "Winning Life's Pageant and Living Well with Diabetes," *Pittsburgh Post-Gazette*, October 25, 2006. www. post-gazette.com/pg/06298/732550-114.stm.

25. Quoted in Michael Silver, "Cutler Adjusting to Life with Diabetes," Yahoo! Sports,

May 16, 2008. www.yahoo.com/news/cutler-adjusting-life-diabetes-162200078--nfl.html.

26. Quoted in Bill Williamson, "Refreshed, Cutler Ready to Tackle Disease, Football, Life," ESPN, May 28, 2008. sports.espn.go.com/nfl/columns/story?id=3416163.

Chapter Five: Diabetes in the Future

27. "Beta Cell Regeneration," Mayo Clinic, accessed July 17, 2017. www.mayo.edu/research/centers-programs/center-regenerative-medicine/focus-areas/beta-cell-regeneration.

28. Asian Scientist Newsroom, "Lab-Grown Pancreas Reverse Diabetes in Mice," *Asian Scientist*, February 8, 2017. www.asianscientist.com/2017/02/in-the-lab/lab-grown-pancreas-reverse-diabetes/.

29. "Pancreatic Islet Transplantation," National Institute of Diabetes and Digestive and Kidney Diseases, September 2013. www.niddk.nih.gov/health-information/diabetes/overview/insulin-medicines-treatments/pancreatic-islet-transplantation.

30. Quoted in Erin Allday, "13,000 in S.F. to Discuss Diabetes Treatments," *San Francisco Chronicle*, June 6, 2008. www.pressreader.com/usa/san-francisco-chronicle/20080606/281539401705804.

31. Production Assistant, "FDA Approves First Artificial Pancreas," Diabetes in Control, October 15, 2016. www.diabetesincontrol.com/fda-approves-first-artificial-pancreas/.

autoimmune disease: A disease in which the body's immune system mistakenly attacks part of the body.

cholesterol: A fatlike substance made by the body and found naturally in foods such as beef, eggs, and dairy products.

diabetic ketoacidosis: A dangerous medical condition in which ketones build up in the blood, which happens when the body is severely low in insulin. This occurs most often in people with type 1 diabetes.

gland: A bodily organ that produces chemical substances for use in the body. One example is the pancreas, which produces insulin.

glucagon: A hormone created in the pancreas that helps the liver release glucose into the bloodstream.

hemoglobin: A red protein that carries oxygen in the blood of vertebrates, or animals with backbones.

hyperglycemic: Having too much glucose in the bloodstream.

hypoglycemic: Having too little glucose in the bloodstream.

ketone: A compound produced when the body uses fats for energy.

neuropathy: A disease or dysfunction of the nerves outside the brain and spinal cord that makes part of the body weak or numb.

obesity: Having a high amount of body fat, making the person more than 20 percent overweight.

psyche: The human mind, soul, or spirit.

Academy of Nutrition and Dietetics
120 S. Riverside Plaza, Suite 2190
Chicago, IL 60606–6995
(800) 877-1600
www.eatright.org
The mission of this organization is to promote optimal nutrition and well-being for all people by advocating for its members.

American Association of Diabetes Educators (AADE)
200 W. Madison Ave., Suite 800
Chicago, IL 60606
(800) 338-3633
www.diabeteseducator.org
AADE is a multidisciplinary organization of more than 14,000 health professionals dedicated to advocating quality diabetes education and care.

American Diabetes Association
2451 Crystal Drive, Suite 900
Arlington, VA 22202
(800) 342-2383
www.diabetes.org
The American Diabetes Association is the nation's leading nonprofit health organization providing diabetes research, information, and advocacy. Founded in 1940, the American Diabetes Association conducts programs in all 50 states and the District of Columbia, reaching hundreds of communities. The mission of the association is to prevent and cure diabetes and to improve the lives of all people affected by diabetes.

Joslin Diabetes Center
One Joslin Pl.
Boston, MA 02215
(617) 309-2400
www.joslin.org
Affiliated with Harvard Medical School, Joslin Diabetes
Center is the world's largest diabetes research center,
diabetes clinic, and provider of diabetes education.

Juvenile Diabetes Research Foundation International
26 Broadway, 14th floor
New York, NY 10004
(800) 533-2873
info@jdrf.org
www.jdrf.org
Driven by the needs of people with diabetes, the
mission of the Juvenile Diabetes Research Foundation
International is to find a cure for diabetes and its
complications through the support of research. It works
to accomplish this by finding and funding the best and
most relevant research to help achieve a cure for this
disease through restoration of normal blood sugar levels,
avoidance and reversal of complications, and prevention
of diabetes and its recurrence.

Books

Betschart-Roemer, Jean. *Type 2 Diabetes in Teens: Secrets for Success*. New York, NY: John Wiley & Sons, 2002.
This book for teens with type 2 diabetes was written to help them and their families understand the illness and how to cope with it. It has a special section of tips and suggestions for parents.

Fuhrman, Joel. *The End of Diabetes: The Eat to Live Plan to Prevent and Reverse Diabetes*. New York, NY: HarperOne, 2014.
This book gives information on how to eat healthy to help manage or prevent diabetes.

Hunter, William. *Nature & Nurture: The Causes of Obesity*. Broomall, PA: Mason Crest, 2015.
Obesity is a major factor in the development of type 2 diabetes. Many people think obesity happens when people are lazy or greedy, but the truth is much more complex. Learning what causes obesity and how to deal with it can help people avoid developing type 2 diabetes and other health conditions.

Moran, Katherine J. *Diabetes: The Ultimate Teen Guide*. Lanham, MD: Scarecrow, 2004.
This book by a nurse and certified diabetes educator, whose daughter was diagnosed with type 1 diabetes when she was three, is an informative guide for teenagers. It discusses both the health and social issues teens with diabetes must deal with.

Scheiner, Gary. *Think Like a Pancreas: A Practical Guide to Managing Diabetes with Insulin.* New York, NY: Marlowe, 2004.
From an author who has diabetes and is also an exercise physiologist and certified diabetes educator, this book offers a clear guide to managing diabetes.

Simons, Rae. *A Kid's Guide to Diabetes.* Vestal, NY: Village Earth Press, 2014.
This book helps children and young adults learn about diabetes and how it can be managed.

Websites

Children with Diabetes
childrenwithdiabetes.com
This online community provides information and support for children with diabetes and their families. Always ask a parent or guardian before participating in an online forum.

***Diabetic Living:* Recipes**
www.diabeticlivingonline.com/diabetic-recipes
The recipes page of this online magazine gives hundreds of healthy, delicious recipes that are approved for people with diabetes.

National Institute of Diabetes and Digestive and Kidney Diseases (NIDDK)
www.niddk.nih.gov/health-information/diabetes
The diabetes page on the NIDDK's website has a wealth of information about this disease, including health tips, basic information, and statistics.

A Sweet Life
asweetlife.org
This online magazine features articles that offer
practical advice, recipes, and information for people
living with diabetes.

**TeensHealth: "My Friend Has Diabetes. How Can
I Help?"**
kidshealth.org/en/teens/friend-diabetes.html#
This article gives clear, helpful information about how
to recognize the signs of a diabetic emergency and how
to support a friend or family member with diabetes in
everyday life.

A

B

C

Traditional Foods Project study of, 50
Children's Hospital Oakland Research Institute, 81
cholesterol, 30, 51, 79
Cleveland, Gerald, 8–9
Cleveland, Robert, 8–9
Colberg, Sheri
on physical and emotional issues, 44
on self-management, 43
on strength from diagnosis, 60
coma, 17, 58
concentrated broccoli sprout extract, 80
cure, 17, 29, 61, 73, 77, 81–83, 85
Cutler, Jay, 8, 70–71

D

death, 8, 10, 15, 19, 58
deoxyribonucleic acid (DNA), 81–82
Department of Health and Human Services, 51
Dexcom, 73–74
Diabetes Daily, 63
diabetes self-management education and support
(DSME/S), 44–45
diabetes, what not to say to someone with, 60–61, 63
diabetic emergencies, 54–56, 59–60, 66
diabetic ketoacidosis (DKA), 28, 58
diabulimia, 47
dietitians, 47
digestion process, 13–14
digestive system, 56
Domi, Max, 8
Dull, Gladys, 9
Duvall, Adam, 8

E

Edison, Thomas, 7

I

immune system, 20, 78–79
immunosuppressive drugs, 79–80
implantable insulin pumps, 37, 39, 83
inactive lifestyle, 17–18
induced pluripotent stem (iPS) cells, 74–75
infections, 15, 20, 28, 42, 79
insulin pumps, 22, 36–38, 63, 69, 73–74, 83–85
insulin resistance, 16, 23
International Diabetes Federation, 10
intestines, 14–15
islets of Langerhans, 78

J

Johnson, Nicole, 67–69
Jonas, Nick, 7, 26
Joslin Diabetes Center
   on finding support groups, 65
   on Halle Berry's diabetes diagnosis, 17
   on insulin pumps, 63
Journal of Diabetes Science and Technology, 53
Juvenile Diabetes Research Foundation, 19–20

K

ketones, 28, 58
kidney failure, 8, 15, 40

L

latent autoimmune diabetes in adults (LADA), 22–23
Latinx, 19, 65
laughter, 59
liver, 15, 40, 56, 78, 80, 83
Lucas, George, 7

W

ABOUT THE AUTHOR

Emily Mahoney is the author and editor of over a
dozen nonfiction books for young readers on various
topics. She has a master's degree in literacy from the
University at Buffalo and a bachelor's degree from
Canisius College in adolescent education and English.
She currently teaches reading to middle school
students and loves watching her students learn how
to become better readers and writers. She enjoys
reading, pilates, yoga, and spending time with family
and friends. She lives with her husband in Buffalo,
New York, where she was born and raised.